'Lauren's book offers a positive and empowering perspective on feminism in Christianity today. Her insightful reflections challenge and inspire, making it a must-read for those seeking a renewed understanding of the intersection of faith and feminism. Lauren beautifully navigates complex topics with grace and wisdom, making this book a valuable contribution to the ongoing conversation about equality and empowerment. A compelling read!'
Charlie Blythe, EU Director of A21

'I regularly found myself pausing for thought while reading this book. Lauren bravely and skilfully tackles hard-hitting women's issues with careful consideration, alternative perspectives and a *brilliantly* sassy sense of humour. I was not expecting a book about feminism and faith to evoke such frequent belly laughs!'
Joanne Bradford, psychotherapist and author of *The Inner Fix*

'Lauren is a funny, provocative and deeply honest guide to any of us who want to explore how our devotion to Jesus can define and embolden our commitment to all that's good and right with feminism. As a Jesus freak and guilty feminist, I love Lauren's unflinching interrogation of where (and why) the Church has held women back from God's call on their lives and her commitment to the wholeness of humanity: women and men. Part manifesto, part testimony, *Notes on Feminism* will stir you to show up with magnificent hope for girls and women in your community.'
Rachel Gardner, Youth Resourcing Lead at St Luke's Blackburn, and author of *The Sex Thing* and *The Girl De-Construction Project*

'*Notes on Feminism* is a superb book. Lauren has written a thorough but thoroughly readable exploration of significant issues that affect us all. Prepare to be informed, challenged and engaged, and to enjoy this important book that both men and women will equally benefit from. This is a book I will be recommending repeatedly to Christians who are grappling with the role of women and men, and how we live more positively as a society together.'
Cathy Madavan, author of *Irrepressible, Why Less Means More* and *Up and Alive*

'If you've ever wondered if it's possible to be both a Christian and a feminist, then this book is for you! Lauren Windle looks at key Bible verses, breaks down taboos with clear arguments, and offers useful advice in her usual chatty style. With experiences of her own and from a range of women, she paints an eye-opening picture of why this subject remains so important in the world of church.'
Revd Jules Middleton, vicar and author of *Breaking the Mould*

'I celebrate how Lauren boldly answers God's call on her life to step out and speak into areas the Church has often sadly shied away from. *Notes on Feminism* is a story-filled, research-packed book that acts as the perfect conversation starter into this important topic. You may not agree with every angle or stance taken, but I encourage you to allow Lauren's words to spark conversation with your friends, church and, most importantly, Jesus. My prayer for women who read this book is that you would feel loved, seen and known by Jesus. And for men, I pray that you would read this book, press in to Jesus, and allow him and his word to shape your heart to love women his way – because God's way is always the best way.'
Andy Monks, author of *The Now Generation* and Head of Children and Youth at Ascension Balham

'Funny for a girl.'
My mate Barney

'Every Christian woman needs to read this book. Lauren has approached the topic with great pastoral sensitivity, thorough journalistic research and her characteristic warmth and wit. Wherever you stand on the spectrum of feminism, I believe there is space for you to wrestle in these pages with Lauren as a gentle and wise guide. In short, buy a copy – and then buy some more for your friends.'

Rachael Newham, author of *Learning to Breathe* and *And Yet*

'Funny, controversial, grace-filled, gritty and thought-provoking... *Notes on Feminism* is all this and more. Lauren curates the open conversation that you'll want to join, so read it and share how you agree, disagree, and all the in-betweens.'

Amy Boucher Pye, author of *Transforming Love* and *7 Ways to Pray*

'The exact book I want both my daughter and son to read when the time comes. Lauren skilfully navigates the hot topic of feminism with loving grace and refreshing candour.'

John Reynolds, influencer and author of *Able To Laugh*

'Lauren Windle is one of my favourite writers. In fact, she might be one of my favourite humans. Part of the reason for this is that she never quite does what you expect. So if you're coming to this book expecting an angry tirade against men and masculinity, think again. What you'll find instead is a collection of brilliant thoughts about women, men, power, justice and faith, drawn together through a journalist's pen and with a stand-up comedian's eye. It's alternately moving, hilarious and thoughtful, and it's definitely not just for women – or even feminists. This might be the most balanced, surprising and open-hearted book on feminism I've ever come across. Written into a world and a subject that's desperately short on nuance, it's a gift.'

Martin Saunders, Director, Satellites Event, and author of *The Man You're Made to Be* and *We Are Satellites*

'Lauren's journalism shines as she compassionately and critically helps us to think through and grasp the breadth of this evolving conversation – not to instruct but to inform. A provoking and timely book handled with grace, and of course a dash of humour, I love how she sensitively creates space for us to draw our own diverse conclusions while retaining our bonds. A must-read for women and men alike.'
Monique Thomas, author of *Pressure Off*

'The way Lauren writes is perfect, bringing a serious topic out into the light with a dash of humour sprinkled throughout. An educational read with practical insight to take forward for people in all areas of society – including male leaders and friends!'
Hope Virgo, founder of #DumpTheScales and author of *You Are Free*

'In *Notes on Feminism*, Lauren Windle skilfully gathers a host of voices and, adding her own insightful, honest and often witty perspectives, encourages us to hold in tension more than one opposing view. These pages are full of the rich, deep and nuanced experiences of women in whose shoes we are invited to walk, so their view of the world can enrich our own. This book imparts knowledge, and that, as the saying goes, is power.'
Arianna Walker, CEO of Mercy UK

Lauren Windle is a journalist, presenter and public speaker, published by *Vogue*, *Marie Claire*, *HuffPost*, *Red* magazine, MailOnline, The Sun online, Fabulous Digital, The Star, *Church Times* and others. She also presents *Third Wheel Dates*, a show on dating app Salt's YouTube channel.

On 22 April 2014, Lauren got clean and sober from a cocaine and alcohol addiction, and became a Christian five days later. She has a degree in Neuroscience and a master's in Addiction Studies, runs a charity recovery course for people struggling with addiction and, in 2018, gave a TEDx Talk about her personal story of addiction and recovery that has been viewed half a million times. She can recite virtually every word of the BBC's 1995 dramatisation of *Pride and Prejudice* by heart and never says no to a Toby Carvery.

You can connect with Lauren @laurenwindle_ on Instagram and Twitter (or 'X', as Elon wants us to call it now).

NOTES ON FEMINISM

Being a woman in a Church led by men

Lauren Windle

First published in Great Britain in 2024

Society for Promoting Christian Knowledge
SPCK Group, The Record Hall, 16–16A Baldwin's Gardens, London, EC1N 7RJ
www.spck.org.uk

British Library Cataloguing-in-Publication Data
A catalogue record for this book is available from the British Library

ISBN 978–0–281–08767–9
eBook ISBN 978–0–281–08768–6

1 3 5 7 9 10 8 6 4 2

Typeset by Fakenham Prepress Solutions, Fakenham, Norfolk, NR21 8NL
First printed in Great Britain by Clays Ltd, Bungay, NR35 1ED
eBook by Fakenham Prepress Solutions, Fakenham, Norfolk, NR21 8NL

Produced on paper from sustainable sources

For Cathie and Rosie,
the women who are always in my corner

Contents

Contents

Introduction

I know what you're thinking: *Lauren? That sounds like a girl's name. Surely she has more important things to do than write a book? Isn't there something that needs whipping up in the kitchen?* Please rest easy knowing that, as I type, my fridge is stocked full of Co-op ready meals that I can make look homemade for the purposes of Instagram.

I'm joking – obviously. Because if you're a person who's picked up a book with the word 'feminism' on the cover, you're already unlikely to be of the 'women in the kitchen' persuasion. What I have found, though, is that women in the Church often don't sit neatly on the 'feminism spectrum'. If there were one, I imagine it would stretch from highly conservative (1) to radical (10). But, in what has come as a surprise to me, I haven't been able to assign a number to any woman I've spoken to. What I've found instead are women who would refuse to take their husband's last name when they got married (8), but believe the traditionally 'feminine' roles around the house fall to them (3). Then there are women who use words like 'patriarchy' and would challenge anyone to a duel if they suggested a woman might be less competent in a job (7.5), but wouldn't feel right worshipping in a church led by a woman (2). This book won't tell you you're wrong. There's too much arguing as it is. But it is likely to present differing views as, even among my own peer group, no two of us are aligned on every single issue.

There's no way of satisfying everyone when writing on such a hot-button topic. When attempting to straddle the secular feminist movement and the Evangelical Church, I will inevitably be too conservative for the former and too radical for the latter.

1

Researching and writing this book has been an exercise in accepting and acknowledging that someone having a different opinion doesn't discount them from the conversation. Dr Sandra Richter, an Old Testament scholar who believes the Bible supports women in church leadership, is clear that she would still serve in a church where she wasn't allowed to speak if that was where God had called her.[1] She stresses that this is not an issue worth splitting the Church over – and it may surprise you to hear that I agree. I would love you to approach this with the same openness. Here, you are reading a collection of thoughts based on lived experience and research – from other contributors as well as me. No one's claiming to have all the answers or to have identified ultimate truth. It's a piece of journalism... not the Bible. I reserve the right to continue listening, reading and wrestling with these topics, and to allow my understanding of them to grow long after this book is published. I hope that my research and thoughts *inform*, rather than *form*, your own.

I've picked up a lot of books on feminism over the years, and every single one has had a cloying, guilt-riddled paragraph in the Introduction confessing the author's privilege and acknowledging blind spots. I find them very cringey. One that sticks out is when Florence Given declares in *Women Don't Owe You Pretty* that sometimes she wants to shave off her flowing blonde locks so she'll no longer benefit from 'pretty privilege'.[2] Oh Flo, even after undergoing the razor, you'd still be pretty, just in a slightly more Natalie-Portman-in-*V-for-Vendetta* kind of way.

Anyway, here's my declaration: I would be delighted to claim 'pretty privilege', but sadly the men on Hinge don't seem to agree. What I can say with complete certainty is that I'm white, I'm middle class, I'm university educated, I'm straight, I'm not trans and I have no disability. I'm currently unmarried and in my thirties, so wouldn't be considered old. In intersectional terms, I intersect nothing. I've thought a lot about this and whether it means I'm not the right person to write this book. A widely published Black female author shared some wise words with my editor during the inception of this project: 'Feminism doesn't look the same, nor is it experienced the same, among different ethnic or socioeconomic groups.' She's completely right.

This imbalance plays out in many, many ways. I am most acutely aware of it when I speak of my experience as a drug addict in recovery. Peer-reviewed research is clear that those with these aforementioned privileges are far more likely to get into and stay in recovery than those without. It's just a horrifically sad fact that we all need to be aware of and continue to challenge until society reflects the kingdom of God.

In order to widen my understanding of different perspectives on feminism, I've asked a diverse group about their experiences of being both a woman and a Christian. As well as speaking to individuals, I've interviewed sisters at a convent and hosted focus groups to discuss key topics. Throughout this book, I'll refer to the All Saints (a group of women from a mix of Anglican and evangelical backgrounds), Westlife (a group of men from Anglican churches) and Sugababes (a group of Baptist women of colour). Yes, I have been listening to a lot of Heart 00s recently. Why do you ask? These three groups are all united in wholeheartedly loving God.

I've also invited five incredible women to contribute a chapter each from their perspective: journalist Delphine Chui, Olympian Abigail Irozuru, author Tiffany Bluhm, presenter and comedian Cassandra Maria, and broadcaster Katie Piper OBE. They each speak of trials, challenges and experiences that I have either not experienced at all or not experienced to the same extent. Like me, they don't speak for everyone of their sex, ethnicity or denomination – just for themselves. There is no book wide enough to cover every topic that affects Christian women and from every potential perspective. So, if you relate to passages here, that's great. But if you don't, it's an opportunity to learn more about the experiences of another person.

As a journalist who researches and writes about things that overlap with my personal experience, I don't feel I have the authority to speak into the lesbian or trans experience. I realise these are extremely complex when they intersect with a faith community that has historically been incredibly and disappointingly unwelcoming. There are other books that are solely dedicated to speaking on these topics, and to write a short chapter addressing either subject when they are so far out of my areas of expertise or experience would be slapdash at best. What I will say is that gay, straight, cis, trans or any other descriptive term – you are wecome here. You should also be welcome in all churches. Regardless of a church leader's stance on any topic in this area, you should always be greeted with open arms into the church community and family of Christ. That's your Father's house, after all.

As a fair bit of this book will be written through the lens of my experience, it would be right to introduce myself properly. I'm Lauren. Christian, recovering addict, journalist, public speaker, presenter, author of *Notes on Love*, Londoner, four times godmother, Gantt chart lover, and fan of Tim Tam Slamming with Penguin bars.

To the men reading this – who are likely to be my mate Sam and (reluctantly) my dad – I hope it doesn't sound accusatory or angry. This is not a call for Christian women to arm themselves with tent pegs. We love you. We value men's input and support, but we just want to redress a balance that can often feel skewed.

To the women reading this – the subject matter is complex and, particularly as we address some of the heavier topics towards the end, you may find it tough. We can read as many mainstream books on feminism as we like, but navigating this movement while being a Christian is different. Sometimes we can feel as if we're torn between rallying with women of the world and doing what God wants for us. We're in a community where a huge number of Protestant churches, and most Catholic ones, don't believe a woman should lead. There are wildly varying views on the roles of men and women in the home. And, generally speaking, the Church's history of supporting female victims has been poor. Many of us are angry, but we have to balance that with a faith that tells us to forgive. We don't know if we should be turning tables or turning the other cheek. We're all just trying our best to understand the complicated text of the Bible and we all land in different places with our beliefs. But for Christians who want to support the plight of women, there's the added question of whether or not we're going against God and the 'natural order of things'. It's incredibly difficult to navigate when the petition for equality is called 'blasphemy' by many. A lot of us are scared that God actually does place less value on women. On expressing all this to my mentor, she said, 'Lauren, God's not on the "wrong" side of this. It's okay to explore it.'

This fear, uncertainty and confusion is exactly why this book is necessary. I know I'm not the only one. So I hope that my research and the various thoughts and opinions in this book will help you unpick any lies you've begun to believe, and ultimately bring you closer to God.

Through these pages we'll look at the language we use around feminism and women in general. We'll address common stereotypes about women's looks and humour. We'll look at what the Bible says about women, and how different people interpret those passages, and we'll address the upset and anger of women who have been mistreated.

There is a lot at play and a lot at stake, and there are many opposing views and interpretations to navigate. It's easy to feel frustrated, guilty, angry and lonely. But you are loved and supported, and definitely not alone. Let's agree that when you finish this book, you'll message someone and ask them to pray for you. Win, lose or draw. Whether you feel better, worse or the same as when you started, reach out to someone and ask them to cover you in prayer. We stand strongest when we stand together in relationship with each other and God – so don't shortchange yourself.

The 'F' word

'Feminism' is a dirty word. You only have to fast-forward two chapters – to where journalist Delphine Chui explains, with words left unminced, why she does not identify with the feminist movement – to see that it conjures negative associations. I don't 100% agree with her; this would be a boring book if I did. But you'll see that she's highlighted a number of key issues that some men and some women struggle with when it comes to identifying with the cause of feminists.

The first thing I started asking Christians when I was developing this book was: 'Do you consider yourself a feminist?' The responses were 50/50. Some said they did – but often with caveats – while others shuddered at the suggestion. One of the All Saints said she was 'a feminist in substance but not in terminology', while a member of Sugababes said she loved the idea of female empowerment but was 'too traditional' to call herself a feminist. Those two statements eloquently sum up how many more felt.

Time after time I heard women defiantly reject 'feminism' as a word that's become too charged, but when I asked them about their views, they would adamantly defend equality and rights for women. Next I dug deeper, doing what any self-respecting millennial with information to gather does – I took to Instagram. I asked followers if they believed you could be a Christian and a feminist. The (predominantly male) respondents asked what I meant by 'feminism'. One dramatically renounced the term, saying that, just like male chauvinism, it was totally 'unbiblical'.

One woman I spoke to was adamant that she couldn't identify with the feminist movement, as she felt it had done too much harm to women of colour. She said: 'I don't see an "all women rise up together" movement. I see white women who rise up together. There's an elitism in feminism and I don't want anything to do with it.'

One of the men from Westlife explained that he would have considered himself a feminist a few years ago, but now fears feminists would think him sexist. He said: 'The word "sexist" has expanded. Before, I never would have said I was sexist, as to my mind that was someone who was deliberately hateful. But now you can be sexist for unconscious bias. I do believe in equality of opportunity for men and women. But I'm not an activist, so passionate feminists would probably say I don't do enough to qualify.'

Let's be real – the majority perspective on feminism looks bleak. For some, the word conjures up pictures of angry, unshaven women taking offence at anything and everything, picking fault with men and setting fire to their own undergarments. Others think of a group of self-righteous white women who claim to fight for everyone, but instead settle for greater opportunities for themselves. In the world and Church as a whole, feminists are branded aggressive and argumentative, naive and oblivious. And by that standard, no one would want to sign up. But what about the women who are joyful feminists who understand a lot of the difficulty around the movement, but would still happily use the term for self-identification? Why aren't people seeing them? It may be time for the term 'feminism' to get a rebrand.

Defining feminism

My feeling is that, when defined properly, we should all be happy to identify with the label 'feminist'. A part of the issue is that, at present, there's just one catch-all word, when really it's an umbrella term covering many different groups and views. Much like there are thousands of denominations that associate with Christianity, so two people describing themselves as 'Christian' doesn't mean they're in complete agreement. There are some who are passionate about the movement, but will use the term 'womanist' in order to distance themselves from the long association with feminism and the priorities of white women.

Many of these subsections of feminism have been defined, and various groups are referenced by different authors and speakers who engage with the movement: gender, equality, liberal, radical, Marxist, cultural, eco, multiracial, intersectional, postmodern and others. I can see how these new branches were developed in the hope of rectifying problems with the previous ideology, but in many cases they have caused further division and disagreement.

Broadly, and I mean very broadly, all feminists are fighting for social, political and economic equality of all people, and for the end of oppression against women, with emphasis on topics that disproportionately affect them: sexual harassment, affordable childcare, unpaid labour, reproductive rights, domestic violence, the treatment of women of colour... and the list goes on.

So far so good. While there may be disagreement among Christians about what constitutes liberation for women, the central idea that men and women are equal in dignity is undeniably biblical: 'So God created mankind in his own image, in the image of God he created them; male and female he created them' (Genesis 1:27).

And yet many don't see faith and feminism as compatible. Christians' experience of women's rights is usually exclusively outside the Church, leaving them to develop their understanding of feminism in complete isolation from their faith. I deeply believe that Christianity *is* a religion that empowers women. Yet for many Christian girls, their understanding of Christianity comes entirely from a series of cultural interpretations of their faith dictated by men hundreds of years ago.

Why Christians don't like feminism

There is a tendency for churches from more conservative traditions to be most vocal about their disapproval of the movement. I recognise that people reading this book will likely be from a range of different backgrounds. But let's all agree that there's no space for the liberal moral high ground attitude, which makes everyone think that anyone who isn't progressive is stuffy and old-fashioned. There are bigoted members at each end of the spectrum (see any Louis Theroux documentary ever), plus we need to bear in mind that every group will have people who seek to use Scripture to confirm their own biases. We may even have to examine that tendency in ourselves. But the vast majority of people who resist feminism and women in church teaching roles do so with a good heart and a deep desire to hold to what they truly believe the Bible instructs. The Presbyterian Church of America, Orthodox traditions, the Christian Missionary Alliance of the Southern Baptists and a lot of the churches in the Newfrontiers network all see a message in Scripture that speaks against women taking up leadership roles in ministry. We never want to be people who allow our perception of God and his mission to be dictated by the cultural norms we see around us. We can't impose our brand of morality on God; we look to be shaped by him.

While I can't speak for everyone, those who oppose feminism often do so because they feel it challenges the Bible's instructions about the roles of men and women. Some verses are frequently referred to in this debate, and 1 Timothy 2:11–15 and 1 Corinthians 14:34–35 are right at the top of the list. These are the passages where Paul writes that women 'should learn in quietness and full submission' and shouldn't be allowed to 'assume authority over a man'. In his first letter to the Corinthians, he said: 'Women should remain silent in the churches.'

Taking these at face value, this is an open-and-shut case. The book is finished – let's take our ball and go home. The End.

But those who support women teaching in the Church read this through a lens of interpretation and context. They don't believe that Paul meant these words to apply to all women of all times and in all cultural contexts. More on this to come.

In 1988, the Council on Biblical Manhood and Womanhood (CBMW) released the Danvers Statement. It was written by several evangelical Baptist leaders and summarised the need for the Council on Biblical Manhood and Womanhood. It suggested that women should push back against the prevailing culture and instead pursue 'biblical womanhood'. It said that, by accepting feminist ideology, Christians were creating a 'threat to Biblical authority as the clarity of Scripture is jeopardized and the accessibility of its meaning to ordinary people is withdrawn into the restricted realm of technical ingenuity'.[1]

A Texan evangelical Christian organisation called Vision Forum Ministries, which petitioned for a return to 'biblical patriarchy', claimed: 'Feminism is an enemy of God and of biblical truth.'[2] It has since been shut down because its leader engaged in some 'serious sins' of the extramarital variety. Stacy McDonald, author of *Passionate Housewives Desperate for God*, said: 'Quite simply, there is no such thing as "Christian feminism". We either embrace the biblical model... or we reject it and plummet over the cliff with the rest of the passengers on the railcar.'[3] While the authors of *Take It Back: Reclaiming biblical manhood for the sake of marriage, family and culture*, Dr Tim Clinton and Max Davis, say: 'Things have gotten so rough for traditional men that they are not merely on the ropes and on the verge of being knocked out; they're on the verge of dying – their voices and influence eliminated, snuffed out, dead.'[4]

There are varying degrees of drama in these statements. I don't believe that the fight for women's equality is the devil's attempt to pull us away from God, and neither did Paul, who counted women among some of his most valuable comrades in his mission to spread the gospel. Neither do I believe that men's influence is being snuffed out. Let's look around ourselves before we say silly things like that.

One of the seminal texts on restoring these 'biblical roles' was *Recovering Biblical Manhood & Womanhood: A response to evangelical feminism* by John Piper and Wayne Grudem. They describe masculine and feminine virtues as follows:

> At the heart of mature masculinity is a sense of benevolent responsibility to lead, provide for and protect women in ways appropriate to a man's differing relationships. At the heart of mature femininity is a freeing disposition to affirm, receive and nurture strength and leadership from worthy men in ways appropriate to a woman's differing relationships.[5]

I do not agree with John Piper's position on what it is to be a biblical man or woman. I don't like the idea that a man's masculinity is defined by how he leads women, or that a woman's femininity is based on how she receives that leadership. In her book *Recovering from Biblical Manhood & Womanhood*, Aimee Byrd says: 'The "heart" of masculinity and femininity provided here is all about male leadership... My aim in life is not to be constantly looking for male leadership... Paul teaches mutual submission among Christians even as he addresses husbands and wives specifically.' She goes on to say that it is not a woman's godly feminine duty to affirm masculinity.[6]

Here we face a conundrum that I will talk you through. I like John Piper and respect a lot of his teaching, but this is an area where we are completely at odds. Does this mean I won't listen to his preaching on other topics? No. That would be cutting off my nose to spite my face. I am able to respect and engage with someone I don't wholly agree with.

Why plenty of other people don't like feminism

Let's look at the common objections to feminism, pausing to consider the perspective at play in these arguments. Don't worry if this exploration leaves you with more questions than answers; holding space for different opinions to co-exist is where I want to start out. This is not an extensive list; I don't have the time to write one and you don't have the time to read it. We've all got lives to lead.

Problem
Feminists hate men. They blame all men for the crimes of a few.

Response
A minority of feminist women hate men, but it's #NotAllFeminists – you see what I did there? At the top end of the scale is Valerie Solanas, the woman who shot Andy Warhol, released a manifesto for the Society for Cutting Up Men (aka SCUM) and suggested that women could move back to humanity if they simply exterminated men.[7] The bulk of feminists don't have genocidal aspirations. The majority care a great deal about men. That said, plenty will feel some anger towards men as a collective because of the crimes of individuals, and because of the general, historical, advantage they have enjoyed. This can leave men feeling as if they have to apologise for their gender and that the culture is well and truly against them. That's just not the case though; the idea is to attain greater cohesion and better opportunities for women, which benefits the whole of society.

Problem
It's political correctness gone mad. I like to call this 'the Fox News argument'. Men don't know what they can and can't say any more. They're terrified of getting cancelled if they so much as give a

woman advice on her career, comment on her outfit or offer to help improve her technique at the gym.

Response
It's easy to say something to *anyone* that makes them feel uncomfortable. We're all products of our environment and are unaware of the struggles others have faced. If you say something that someone else corrects you on, reflect on it, hear their explanation, ask yourself if you are able to see things from their perspective and adjust accordingly. Don't plough on with your up-to-the-line joke when someone has made it clear that you've actually crossed that line. Be open to hearing feedback. This is the age of learning for all of us, and we'll move much more swiftly without defensiveness. Here's a cheeky starter for ten: unless she directly asks you, a woman doesn't want your career advice, opinion on her outfit or help at the gym.

Problem
Women have everything – what more could they want? Women can vote, work, learn and own property; they can do everything a man can do these days. Surely there's no need for feminism. We're equal.

Response
So much has changed for women, and we all see that. We are grateful to the women and men who fought for us to have legal rights, and the improvements to our opportunities are too vast to mention. But there is more that can be done. One of the men in Westlife said: 'I am a feminist because even in the heart of a city, in a community that would be described as "progressive" by the majority of Christians, I still see deep inequality and many social structures that restrict or oppress women.'

In a less measured way, second-wave feminist Germaine Greer said:

What more could women want? Freedom, that's what. Freedom from being the thing looked at rather than the person looking back. Freedom from self-consciousness. Freedom from the duty of sexual stimulation of jaded male appetite, for which no breast ever bulges hard enough and no leg is ever long enough.[8]

Gear up for more Greer quotes. Not because I completely agree with her, but because that woman cracks me up.

Problem
Feminism forces women to feel guilty if they don't 'have it all'. Suddenly feminism has swept in and made women who choose to stay at home and raise their children feel like unintelligent, unambitious housewives who just want to wear pinnies and bake pies. It's no longer about giving women the right to decide on their path, but about making them feel guilty if they don't choose *every* path.

Response
Every choice in life involves sacrifices; for any career or school or partner you choose, there are thousands or even millions that you don't. Everyone knows this – even if it fills us with a sense of existential dread. The choice to make being a stay-at-home mum your full-time career, whether temporarily or for the long term, is a complicated one that can be based on your financial situation, the structure of your family, available childcare and preference. I'm not a fan of the *expectation* that a woman should leave her job and stay at home, just as I'm not a fan of the *expectation* that she should arrange alternative care and go back to her job. Feminism is about expanding a woman's options, not forcing her into one. Whether she goes back to her job or not, she will be working twenty-four hours a day for a long time. I truly believe both decisions are

incredibly challenging – physically, emotionally and mentally – and new parents need our support, care and prayer rather than our judgement.

Problem

Women aren't able to disagree with feminism. Feminists will sometimes speak of this experience when something 'clicks' and suddenly a woman's eyes are opened to the subjugation and inequality around her. This attitude – that some women are waiting for their awakening – can seem to make it impossible to debate the opinions of feminists. This was flagged by British philosopher Sir Karl Popper and explained by Christina Hoff Sommers in her book *Who Stole Feminism?*:

> Gender feminism is *nonfalsifiable*, making it more like a religious undertaking than an intellectual one. If, for example, some women point out that *they* are not oppressed, they only confirm the existence of a system of oppression, for they 'show' how the system dupes women by socializing them to *believe* they are free, thereby keeping them docile and cooperative.[9]

Feminist Naomi Wolf took every woman who publicly disagreed with her work as further proof of how engrained patriarchy is in the minds of women, and spoke of how troubling she found it when women denied their oppression.[10]

Response

If a woman doesn't feel hurt by the systems around her and doesn't feel that she's been oppressed or subjugated in any way by men or society, that's great. It's probably a much happier place to be in than feeling constantly on the lookout for the next example of oppression. It could be that she's not seeing it, or it could be that it's just not there. I'm not here to create problems. It's arrogant to assume that someone who doesn't see things your way isn't sufficiently aware. Let's give everyone the credit they deserve, allowing them to think through the issues and characterise their own experiences accordingly.

Problem

Feminists make everything harder work. Picking at every system and suggesting ways they can be more 'inclusive' is such a headache for everyone. Things are fine, women have legal rights now. Do we have to dismantle everything? We're all sick of angry women complaining about small things.

Response

What is and isn't small looks very different, depending on how close you are to it. It's a matter of perspective. I think when looking at making changes that may or may not be positive in a company, church or society, it's important to ask ourselves: who benefits? Who benefits from us doing the work to make those changes, and who doesn't? Who benefits from the outcome of those changes, and who doesn't? If keeping it simple and leaving things as they are benefits people who are already in positions of power, and making changes could lead to a more diverse distribution of that power among people who previously didn't have access to it, then I would think very carefully about opposing doing that 'harder work'. Jesus was in favour of the oppressed.

Problem

Feminists see everything as sexism. Sometimes someone's rude to you because you're annoying. Not because you're a woman. Sometimes you didn't get the job because you weren't qualified enough. Not because you're a woman. Sometimes someone patronises you just because they're an idiot. Not because you're a woman.

Response

I've seen examples of this that I agree with. The main one that springs to mind is when Susan McClary, PhD, Professor of Musicology, said that the music of Beethoven's ninth symphony mirrors the rage of a rapist incapable of attaining release. Christina Hoff Sommers, who wrote about this in *Who Stole Feminism?*, said: 'Once I get into the habit of regarding women as a subjugated gender, I'm primed to be alarmed, angry, and resentful of men as oppressors of women. I am also prepared to believe the worst about them and the harm they cause to women.'[11]

But while I agree that ridiculous extremes are sometimes drawn, and it isn't sexism *every* time, I also, really sadly, think that more poor behaviour towards women is in some way influenced by societal oppression than many people realise. Asking yourself the question, 'Would that person have done/said that if they were interacting with a man?', often casts new light on the situation.

Problem

Feminists are too angry. Feminists are women who are unhappy because they can't find a husband or got passed over for a job or got sick of shaving their legs every day.

Response

Sometimes it's okay to be angry. Well-directed anger has historically changed the world. Before you judge someone for being 'too angry', I think it's important to remember that you don't know their life story and why they have the ferocity they bring to a situation. People who are scared can respond in anger. If everyone felt honoured, supported, heard and loved, there would be far less anger knocking about.

Why so many people who aren't white don't like feminism

In my Sugababes focus group, one woman said: 'There is no "white" feminism. As far as I can see, all feminism is white feminism. We're all image-bearers of Christ, but feminism doesn't seem to give us the same dignity, and that elitism plays out in the Church too.' Contributors to Muslim book *It's Not About the Burqa* said they felt that 'people from different cultures can be "othered" in a [feminist] movement that should represent all women'.[12]

This is particularly disappointing for women of colour, given that many experts in the field suggest that patriarchy and white supremacy are two sides of the same coin. In her book *The Making of Biblical Womanhood*, Beth Allison Barr says:

> Patriarchy walks hand in hand with racism, and it always has. The same biblical passages used to declare Black people unequal are used to declare women unfit for leadership. Patriarchy and racism are 'interlocking structures of oppression.' Isn't it time we got rid of both?[13]

John MacArthur, a prominent evangelical pastor, appeared in a widely shared video in 2019, criticising Southern Baptist Convention leaders for their suggestion that there should never be another Bible translation committee without a Latina, Black or female scholar on it. His comment was: 'Translation of the Bible? How about someone who knows Greek and Hebrew?'[14] Note that there was never a suggestion that any old woman of colour should be invited to join, but a scholar – someone fully qualified to contribute. Sadly, there are plenty more examples, both anecdotally and statistically, where we see people exercising racism and patriarchy in heartbreaking ways. There are many through the pages of this book. For a full and detailed dive into the intersection of race and sex in the Church, I highly recommend Chine McDonald's *God Is Not a White Man*, which is a powerful and thought-provoking deep-dive into the experience of people who aren't white and male, based on Chine's thorough research and lived experience.[15]

What feminism *could* be

These concerns lie beneath the many different divisions and subgroups of feminism. They explain why so many people resist the idea of identifying with the feminist movement – and I totally get it. There are a lot of writers and speakers who have chosen their own word; one they feel relates to their ideas better than the stigmatised word 'feminism'.

Some people say they are on the side of 'sameness' or 'fairness'. Christy Bauman, author of *Theology of the Womb*, describes herself as a 'womanist' rather than a feminist.[16] Others say they want equality or justice. For a long time I saw these as synonymous, but the more I think about it, the more I feel they're not.

I'm 5ft 3, right, so I'm pretty short. Say I'm walking down the street with my mate Ross, who's 6ft 3, and we realise there's a parade on the other side of a long fence. The fence is six foot, so he can see what's going on but I can't. In this scenario, equality would be giving both of us a half-foot-high box to stand on to help us see over. But if you did that, I would still be staring at the fence and he would have an even better view. Justice would be giving me both boxes.

I don't believe that God treats us equally. I believe he offers more support and guidance to those who are in greater need. That's what I've seen modelled in Jesus, and I believe we should do the same. With our limited perspectives and human levels of wisdom, working out what is truly *just* in a situation is incredibly challenging. Which is why, a lot of the time, we settle for what is *equal* instead. Of course, I don't believe that God's justice in response to patriarchy is the reciprocal subjugation of men.

At the moment, many Christians are critical of feminism, and many feminists are critical of Christianity. I believe that the two are compatible in far more ways than most people realise. In an article for *Relevant* magazine, writer Amy R. Buckley says:

> How do we address secular feminist concerns? What will we do to create hospitality to feminists in churches? Whether or not we call ourselves Christian feminists, God calls us to be lights in a crooked, messed up world (Philippians 2:15). Opportunities for responding to feminist concerns are great; hopefully the workers won't be few.[17]

All my research, interviews and, well, general life experience has led me to a place where I believe it's time for us to rethink feminism. I haven't come up with a whole new term to define the type of feminism *I'm* talking about. And if you don't want to use the word 'feminism' I don't care – the semantics are unimportant to me, as long as you're championing women and calling out injustice. To me, feminism is empowering all women to have equal opportunities and achievements with men through God's justice. I believe Christians are called to play a part in this, as Christ was not just representative of *male* humanity but of *all* humanity while he was here on earth. As St Augustine asserted: 'It's not just men that are made in the image of God, but women too.'[18]

There are dangers built into hierarchical structures that promote the power of men. As a consequence, virtually every woman has suffered in some way, whether big or small. Authors of *Half the Sky: How to change the world*, Nicholas D. Kristof and Sheryl WuDunn, point out: 'It appears that more girls have been killed in the last fifty years, precisely because they were girls, than men were killed in all the battles of the twentieth century.'[19]

As Christians, we are part of one body. We are a community with vastly different beliefs, especially when it comes to the role of women. The enemy wants separation, because the Church and Jesus' followers are powerful when they pull together. Kat Armas, author of *Abuelita Faith*, says: 'Injustice affects both the oppressor and the oppressed, so we must tell the truth about the past – and the ways we have disrupted our sacred belongingness – so we may heal our future.'[20] Let's pull together and heal. Let's hear each other out and remember that what unites us is far stronger and more powerful than that which would pull us apart.

Feminism: an incomplete – and tongue-in-cheek – history

In the beginning... The first woman, an admittedly rocky start

Eve, the first woman, was created by God as it was 'not good for man to be alone'. Her desperation to get her five-a-day, and her defiance of God in doing so, caused the fall. Ever since, she has been branded 'the original evil woman', kicking off a legacy of wariness towards women and the corrupting influence their feminine wiles can have on men.

Around 350 BC – Aristotle bowls in

In ancient Greece, Plato's trainee Aristotle diagnosed the female condition as a 'deformity'. He said that the female was a 'mutilated male' whose development was stopped early because the coldness of the mother's womb overcame the heat of the father's semen.[1] But then he also thought the earth was the centre of the universe and that men had more teeth than women, which isn't the case. He did have a wife, so it seems like laziness that he didn't check.

Around AD 30 – Jesus pushes back

The Son of God rocked up to sort out the mess humans had made of the earth. He was radical in his approach to women, assigning them far more dignity than the Greco-Roman norms of the day did. This was a culture that said women were inferior to men and shouldn't have direct access to religious teaching. It was decreed that a woman who committed adultery or drank alcohol could face the death penalty. Families didn't even give individual names to their daughters; they were simply assigned the feminine form of their father's name, and if there were multiple girls the subsequent siblings would be numbered. That would make me 'Two' (and not in a cute Six-from-*Blossom* or Thirteen-from-*House* way). But Jesus came to call out the hypocrisy in the way women were treated, and after his resurrection he appeared to women first.

Around AD 50 – Eurotrip

The first European person was converted to Christianity in around AD 50 – and it was a woman. In Acts, Paul dreamed that a Macedonian man was crying out to him, begging him to speak about Jesus in Europe. So like Captain Jack Sparrow in search of rum, he hopped on a boat. When he got there, he realised this Macedonian man was actually a woman named Lydia. The first ever Christian church in Europe met in Lydia's house in Philippi.

Around AD 500 – the accidental bishop

Brigid of Kildare signed up to consecration, but the presiding bishop made a boo-boo and read the episcopal orders (the wrong bit of liturgy), accidentally ordaining her a bishop. On spotting his error, he announced: 'This virgin alone in Ireland will hold the episcopal ordination.' Goodness knows why her sex life (or lack thereof) needed to be highlighted. Bishop Brigid toured Ireland, performing miracles and blessing houses. There may not be a day dedicated to getting drunk in her honour, but at the time she enjoyed spiritual equality with St Patrick himself.

1740–1860 – the industrial revolution

In Britain, the introduction of machinery in farming and other industries meant the workforce changed for good, with women suddenly employed in the mines and in textile factories. And so the gender pay gap was born. Working-class men were paid ten shillings a week for their labour and their female counterparts were given five.

1840–1930 – riding the first wave

First-wave feminism fought for the right to female suffrage – that is, voting in political elections – along with other legal rights, such as filing for a divorce, and rights over their children. There are many key milestones to note in the movement, such as the Seneca Falls Convention in the US, in July 1848 – the first to discuss women's rights. In the UK, most of the action was between 1902 – when a delegation of female textile workers handed a petition with 37,000 signatures to Parliament, demanding the vote for women – and 1918, when women of over thirty who owned property were allowed to vote. This was approximately 40% of the female population. Unlike in other countries, the law didn't exclude women of colour – but the homeowner condition disqualified the vast majority anyway, as they were likely to be part of lower socioeconomic groups that didn't own property. The law was updated to include women equally with men in 1928.

My assumption is that everyone reading this book, male or female, feminist-identifying or not, agrees with the principles of first-wave feminism. If you don't, you're really not going to enjoy the rest of this, and perhaps you should read something else to get you up to speed first (start simple with Chimamanda Ngozi Adichie's *We Should All Be Feminists* (London: Fourth Estate, 2014)).

1960–1980 – riding the second wave

Names like Gloria Steinem, Betty Friedan, Audre Lorde, Simone de Beauvoir and Germaine Greer led the way in the second big push for women's rights. There are many great things about second-wave feminism, including access to colleges and technical schools for women, and allowing women to get mortgages and credit cards without needing a man's co-signature. Before it, employers were able to fire women for getting pregnant, and there was no legal recourse for victims of domestic and sexual assault. Many of them are no longer household names, but we have a huge amount to thank these women for.

The first I knew of Germaine Greer was when she went into the *Celebrity Big Brother* house and promptly walked back out again five days later. I banked her in my encyclopaedic mental record of reality TV participants and didn't think about her again until I started reading up on feminism. Her seminal text, *The Female Eunuch*, published in 1970, was one I decided I had better read. Punches are not pulled. I would characterise her tone as 'pretty peeved'. How about this quote for a bit of a laugh: 'If you think you are emancipated, you might consider the idea of tasting your blood – if it makes you sick, you've a long way to go, baby.'[2]

In many ways – that one especially – I disagree with Germaine. Elements of her prose definitely promote female superiority, which I don't subscribe to. But it was fascinating to identify the seedling that produced the feminist stereotype of hating bras. According to Germaine, the way to stop men from fantasising about breasts was to ditch bras so blokes were forced to get used to their natural shape. She said: 'The only way that women can opt out of such gross handling is to refuse to wear undergarments which perpetuate the fantasy of pneumatic boobs.'[3]

Another interesting point to note is that, if you listen to the audiobook, Germaine reads every quote in the accent of its originator.

It's an unexpected addition, although I didn't realise Freud was Pakistani.

1984 – Bell the babe

Bell Hooks published her book *Feminist Theory: From margin to center* and kick-started the conversation on intersectional feminism. She critiqued second-wave feminism for being white and centred around the middle classes, arguing that it undermined the possibility of feminist solidarity across racial lines. She clarified that feminism is not about working for equality with men, as:

> Women in lower-class and poor groups, particularly those who are non-white… [know] that men in their groups do not have social, political, and economic power, they would not deem it liberatory to share their social status… From the very onset of the women's liberation movement, these women were suspicious of feminism precisely because they recognized the limitations inherent in its definition. They recognized the possibility that feminism defined as social equality with men might easily become a movement that would primarily affect the social standing of white women in middle- and upper-class groups while affecting only in a very marginal way the social status of working-class and poor women.[4]

1970 onwards – the rise of the machines

The digital revolution, or third industrial revolution, materially changed many industries and places of work. Most sectors became based on the exchange of knowledge or services that didn't require any significant physical strength. Suddenly, men and women were equally capable of filling many roles.

1992 – expensive lady vicars

The Church of England finally passed a motion allowing women to be ordained as priests. It took nineteen years and there were just two votes in it. As a result, 430 members of the clergy resigned from their positions and claimed compensation, which cost the Church an estimated £26 million.[5] It was twenty-two years later, in 2014, that the General Synod voted in favour of allowing women to become bishops.

1995–2010 – riding the third wave

The third-wavers had more money and greater professional status, thanks to the efforts of women from the second wave. This allowed them more influence for their causes. Third-wave feminism is designed to be the most open of all, taking into account the marginalised voices second-wave feminists didn't engage with, and this is where factions have split off. There is now a different subset of feminists for every variation of ideology and diversity.

This new iteration seeks to challenge and redefine classic ideas that the media have projected about womanhood, gender, beauty, sexuality, femininity and masculinity. Its proponents fight the patriarchy with irony and respond to acts of violence with inspiring stories of survival.

This is the feminism of *The Vagina Monologues* and, a bit more flippantly, *Sex and the City*. It's girl power and Disney princesses who don't need a man. Third-wave feminism has come under heavy criticism, with some labelling it 'extreme' or 'too radical' (although all iterations of feminism have been accused of radicalism in their day, so it's important to make your own mind up). Some have questioned whether the emphasis on sexualised behaviour and wearing revealing clothes are actually sexual liberation or just a new way of expressing old oppressions.

2012–present day – there's a fourth wave now?

Unbeknown to me before I started my research for this book, there's now a fourth wave – excellent conditions for surfers out here. Some don't agree that it's a thing. But for those who do, it started in 2012 with the unimaginably cruel and violent gang rape of twenty-two-year-old Jyoti Singh in India, who later died of her injuries. The world erupted in international outrage, and protests were held around the globe. Part of this wave were the women's marches in response to Trump's running in, and winning, the US presidential election of 2016. Feminists objected to his candidacy due to a number of sexist incidents surrounding the president, the most memorable of which was his strategy for courting women: 'I don't even wait. And when you're a star they let you do it. You can do anything. Grab them by the pussy. You can do anything.'[6] Charming.

The most significant element of this modern wave was the #MeToo movement,[7] which started in 2006 to support survivors of sexual violence, particularly women of colour. But it really kicked off in 2017, when a slew of famous women came forward to report powerful producer Harvey Weinstein's large-scale sexual harassment of women in the film industry. People all over the world took to social media to share their stories of sexual assault in solidarity. In the first twenty-four hours, Twitter reported that #MeToo had been used more than 825,000 times, while on Facebook 4.7 million people globally had used the hashtag across 12 million posts.

Why I'm not a feminist

DELPHINE CHUI

Delphine Chui is an award-winning journalist, Catholic content creator and founder of befriending charity CareDogs.

As a budding women's magazine journalist, I enthusiastically bought into the idea of feminism in my twenties. I literally had the T-shirt and made countless jokes about taking down the patriarchy. Popular culture was telling me how hard it was to be a woman and I believed it – which, ironically, was what actually made my lived experience difficult.

Instead of embracing my femininity, I saw it as a weakness, feeling that I needed to constantly do and experience more to *be* more. In today's 'cancel culture', where every statement has to be prefaced with a million disclaimers, I'm aware that my decision to ditch feminism (when I reverted back to my faith at thirty) was a controversial one. But I can honestly say that I never realised just how loved, equal and dignified women are – and should be – until I studied the Catholic Bible.

In God's word, women are revered. It is a woman, the Blessed Virgin Mary, who becomes Jesus' first tabernacle, fulfilling Old Testament prophecies and becoming the new ark (Mary's womb) of the covenant (Jesus). The woman at the well evangelises to the Samaritans and beyond after her encounter with Jesus. And Mary Magdalene is the first person visited by the resurrected Jesus. These stories are not few and far between in Scripture. There is such a rich history of women in the Bible who use their feminine gifts to provide care (Martha and Priscilla), counsel (Deborah and Esther),

29

financial support (Joanna and Susanna) and to stand up for what is right (Jael and Judith).

The catechism helps to contextualise scriptural teachings for the everyday, with paragraph 1935 stating:

The equality of men rests essentially on their dignity as persons and the rights that flow from it: Every form of social or cultural discrimination in fundamental personal rights on the grounds of sex, race, color, social conditions, language, or religion must be curbed and eradicated as incompatible with God's design.[1]

Acknowledging the dignity that every human being possesses, paragraph 1947 goes on to say: 'The equal dignity of human persons requires the effort to reduce excessive social and economic inequalities. It gives urgency to the elimination of sinful inequalities.'[2] Due to the hardness of hearts and societal 'norms' of the time, women's equal rights were needed back in the suffragette days – as was divorce during the time of Moses, when husbands were literally killing their wives to be able to remarry under God's supposed law. This all happens under God's permissive will, but it certainly isn't his perfect design.

Modern feminism doesn't make me feel equal. I felt pressured to wrongly overcorrect by distorting my views and trust of men as I started to believe I was emotionally and intellectually superior. I began to believe my worth was purely achievement-based, leading me into an unsustainable cycle of toxic productivity. I was always chasing the next promotion and pursuing side hustles, at the expense of embracing my God-given identity as his daughter. In desperately trying to be a part of the movement, I put aside my own original dream of having a family.

British politician Ann Widdecombe once said: 'It wasn't that we would become men. Instead of civilising the world, what we have done is create a ladette culture. It's true we have certain characteristics that we can bring to the world that are valuable, and shouldn't be submerged.'[3] While men and women are 100% equal in value and dignity (Galatians 3:28), we are not the same. I believe we have differences when it comes to our physical strengths, our emotional capabilities, and our God-designed roles in society and in the family.

The latest wave of feminism is divisive, and I feel it plays down our need for both women and men in society and in the family. The true building block of society, after all, is parenthood. Rightly educating the next generation is the most powerful way to improve the world, but I believed the worldly lie that I needed to 'tick things off' before even thinking of pursuing this.

I started to ask myself: are women really only valued for what they do in society rather than within their families? After all, women thriving in roles as wives and mothers isn't only enough, but essential. As a mixed-race daughter of two immigrants, I grew up constantly being told how difficult my life must be. But the only difficulty I experienced was getting trapped on the treadmill of trying to be a great employee, daughter, sister, friend and girlfriend all at the same time. I didn't even have the capacity to imagine adding wife and mother to that list. No wonder so many of us feel like failures.

Do we not believe that our gift of femininity is equal in value to manhood? Is there something wrong with us if we want to be stay-at-home mums or thrive doing jobs that require homemaking skills? Feminism made me feel I needed to reject learning the useful skills my grandmother had, and focus instead on making money and a name for myself. I believed this to be 'progress', but it simply ended up making me materialistic and distracted.

The only thing I was nurturing was my own narcissism. I believe that when we obsess about a false and competitive ideal of equality rather than complementarity, we lose the reality of what a relationship consists of: a giver and a receiver. Believing that both parties need to be receiving at the same time, all the time, makes everything transactional and not relational. It becomes about 'what I get out of this', and this attitude, a result of my understanding of feminism, was seeping into all my friendships and interactions.

The peak of the sexual revolution and feminist liberation movement in the 1960s was a huge challenge for women, and one we're still suffering the repercussions of today. In my opinion, this didn't make us equal; it just encouraged societal behaviours that pushed out traditional family values, resulting in lots of heartbreak and suffering. Pope John Paul II spoke out about this and encouraged women to make a new movement of feminism, which he coined the 'feminine genius'. According to his 1995 *Letter to Women*, women's unique qualities include receptivity (an active receiving of the gifts of life and love), sensitivity (our intuitive ability to notice the needs of others), generosity (placing value on the human person in a unique way) and maternity (the capacity to sustain and bring forth new life, both physically and spiritually, which makes all women, whether biological mothers or not, especially people-centred).

In his 'Letter to the Bishops of the Catholic Church on the Collaboration of Men and Women in the Church and in the World', Cardinal Joseph Ratzinger, who would later become Pope Benedict XVI, said that the gender war encourages a blurring of the distinctions, and that the differences between men and women 'tend to be denied, viewed as mere effects of historical and cultural conditioning'.[4] As an anthropology graduate and a Christian, I couldn't agree with him more.

Studying history shows me how Russian revolutionary Vladimir Lenin was very open about his mission to destroy the family by pushing women into the workforce. I believe Marxists were able to double the number of labourers, keep wages down, raise the number of people being taxed and encourage the raising of our children to be outsourced. Ironically, this made women more dependent on the state and downplayed our crucial part in creating independence and freedom for our families through self-sufficient and peaceful homes that act as sanctuaries from the outside world.

I certainly got hoodwinked into believing I only had power if it were equal to that of a man. I would love to see a world where women are empowered through work both inside and outside the home. A world where we realise God made us man and woman, in his own image and likeness, for a reason. My post-feminist life has been a real social adjustment. No longer do I engage in belittling jokes about men, see my glass as half empty or believe we need to raise women's rights above those of innocent children or men.

I now embrace my strengths and weaknesses, encourage chivalry, dress femininely and reject the pithy slogan that 'the future is female'. Without men and women, there is no future. Living in this glass-half-full mindset has been life-changing. It's stopped me from seeing others – men and women – as competition to my resources or value, because I know none of that is earned anyway, but rather all a God-given gift. True, authentic femininity means having a sisterhood that reveres all women, just as the Bible does in all its stories of the different paths of women. I refuse to conform to a modern, culturally defined idea of what being a 'good woman' means or believes. And if not identifying as a feminist, and rejecting the ideas that come with it, makes me an 'anti-woman' (as I've been called), then it's pretty clear to me that feminism, as it stands now, is no longer about women anyway.

Women in pain

As a teenager, I remember having regular debates with my male friends about which is more painful – being kicked in the balls or giving birth; one of philosophy's many unanswerable questions. With no understanding of either, I loyally stuck with the women, while every pubescent lad who had ever been the victim of a nutmegging-gone-wrong begged to differ.

Those boys have now grown into men, and plenty have children, so I imagine they will have re-evaluated their answer. One of my male friends' wives, who had just given birth, told me she couldn't believe it was possible to be in that much pain and not die. So that sounds fun.

Women's bodies are spectacularly adept at absorbing pain. I'm sure men's are too, but in the cycle of life they are subjected to far less. Studies suggest women are more sensitive to pain than men, and the way they experience that pain is different. Plus, a woman's sensitivity changes with her menstrual cycle. I believe I have a high pain threshold, but my sister, who is a mother of four, regularly reminds me that I don't know what pain is. I get a similar response when I announce how tired I am.

Arguably the most pain I've ever been in was in 2019. It was a chilly January weekend and, in an attempt to build ecclesiastical sorority, I had invited five women from church to my parents' place in Devon. I had planned a weekend of hilly walks and pub lunches by open fires. As I pushed my trolley around Tesco in Totnes, stocking the fridge before everyone arrived, my stomach started to cramp. I assumed it would pass, so continued down the frozen food aisle to grab a nut loaf for the vegetarian – there's always one. I found myself having to pant, as if I were in the early stages of labour just to accommodate the pain. When two of my friends arrived at the train station, I had to hand over the car keys to one who was fully comp, because I was bent double and couldn't drive.

I lay down in bed, but quickly realised I needed medical attention, so I went to the local GP, who sent me straight to the Gastroenterology unit at the nearest hospital, with a letter saying I had suspected appendicitis and should be seen immediately. By the time I got there, accompanied by my friend, I was in agony. I lurched into a side room, where I was told to wait for a nurse. It was eight o'clock. That's nurse changeover time, so no one was in a hurry to tend to me. I couldn't get comfortable, so I crouched on the floor in a child's pose with my arms out above my head, gripping on to my friend's hands with all my might. I was screaming.

A male surgeon came in to speak to me. He agreed that I should have some pain relief and said he would ask a nurse to arrange it. He asked if I could be pregnant. I said I wasn't. He said he'd check anyway, because: 'You never know, do you?' I wanted to tell him that if the pregnancy test came back positive he shouldn't bother calling a nurse, but get the Pope on the phone instead, but I was in too much pain to be sassy. A nurse came in to collect some vital statistics and provide me with painkillers. She asked how I would rate my pain on a scale of 1 to 10. I said 8, but the surgeon interrupted and said to the nurse: 'Put 5. If you write 8 they'll run her straight into surgery.'

She ignored him and wrote 8, but sadly they did not rush me straight into surgery – more's the pity. The analgesics provided enough relief for me to lie down on the stiff blue bed lined with large kitchen roll. At this point a second nurse, this time male, came for a chat and explained that they wanted to hold off taking action until I'd had a scan, and see if anything in my bloods had changed before operating. I was staying in overnight and would be kept comfortable while they waited. Apparently, the surgeon felt that although appendicitis was possible, it was probably a problem with my 'lady parts'. He wasn't specific, but I assumed he wasn't referring to my Shellac nails. I explained that, at the age of thirty-one, I was familiar with what pain in my 'lady parts' felt like and I hadn't experienced anything like this before, but to no avail.

A full day passed, with the same surgeon insisting we 'wait to see how it plays out'. There was a backlog of people in the queue for scans, so I wasn't given one, and at 8 p.m. the following day I was told I may as well eat something as I wouldn't be going into surgery. I crammed down one triangle-shaped quarter of a cheese sandwich and then resumed my bent-double position on the bed, praying for the sweet relief of an Oramorph top-up. Which, as a recovering addict, I was given sparingly.

After the shift change, a female surgeon came to speak to me. She spent all of thirty seconds next to my bed, watching me writhe around in pain, before saying they would be taking me into surgery as soon as six hours had passed since my last meal. I was so relieved I cried, and she gave me a hug. I had my appendix removed at 3 a.m., and the doctors told me afterwards it was one of the worst they had seen. It had burst like a sealed tin of beans in a microwave.

In the morning, when the consultant did his rounds, he was joined by my 'problem with your lady parts' surgeon and by my guardian angel surgeon. Seeing me in a post-op bed, the male surgeon announced, 'Well, this was a surprise to us all.' I ignored him and mouthed, 'Thank you,' to the woman who had stepped in. She mouthed back, 'You're welcome.' And I wanted to cry all over again.

I thought of writing an email to the hospital to complain, but I didn't. And just over a year later a global pandemic kicked in, so it won't have been all sunshine and rainbows for him. I'm sure the mandatory changing of PPE after every toilet break stung far more than my strongly worded feedback would have.

Sadly, this kind of experience is not uncommon. The dismissing and patronising of women who report pain is well documented. It was back in 1982 that a study by nursing professor Joan Crook and psychiatrist Eldon Tunks found that women were far more likely to be misdiagnosed with a mental health condition than men when consulting physicians about chronic pain.[1] Another study found that women who received coronary bypass surgery were only half as likely to be prescribed painkillers as men who had undergone the same operation.[2] Plus women in the US were found to wait on average sixty-five minutes before receiving prescribed relief for acute abdominal pain in A&E, compared to forty-nine minutes for men.[3] Chronic pain sufferers are 70% female, but 80% of the studies have been conducted on men.[4]

Back in the seventies, Germaine Greer wrote: 'It was assumed that unmarried women and widows suffered most from hysteria, and that a good husband could fix it.'[5] In the book *Invisible Women*, Caroline Criado Perez points out: 'Women's reports of physical pain are far more likely to be diagnosed as depression or psychosomatic. Eighties and nineties studies showed that when men reported pain they were more likely to receive pain medication and women were more likely to receive sedatives or antidepressants.'[6] All I can picture is a frantic Mrs Bennet from *Pride and Prejudice* 'taking to her bed', in desperate need of smelling salts. Even in the Bible, Hannah isn't taken seriously in her emotional pain – Eli accuses her of being drunk (1 Samuel 1:13). Or, in a less highbrow example, Angela in *The Office* (US) complains that her boss Michael Scott always wants to know when the women are on their periods, to which he replies: 'I have to know how seriously to take you.'

I hear this story over and over again from friends who have been sent away from A&E for overreacting about their 'period pain', only to be diagnosed with endometriosis at some point down the line. Another classic is fibromyalgia, a widespread condition that causes chronic pain in muscles, joints and ligaments, as well as debilitating fatigue. Tabitha McDuffee wrote about her battle to get diagnosed for *Christianity Today* in 2018. She said that after four years and multiple medical professionals implying it was 'all in her head', she finally received a diagnosis.[7] No one is completely sure why the disease comes on, but it is usually triggered by an acute illness, surgery, or physical or psychological trauma, and 80% of patients are female. Survivors of rape are three times more likely to have the condition, and it has a high prevalence in female veterans. In 2016, a study of 384 Syrian refugee women found that around 30% exhibited symptoms of severe fibromyalgia, compared to 2% of American women.[8] I am capable of showing my fair share of sass now and again, and, while Tabitha is Arab–American, English is her first language and she is a brilliant communicator – yet neither of us was believed. So what chance does a female refugee stand; someone who doesn't necessarily have a good grip on hospital systems and struggles to speak the language?

This is another area where the situation is exacerbated if you are not white. A 2016 study found that Black patients were about half as likely to be prescribed opioid medicines in the emergency department than white patients reporting the same amount of pain.[9] Another study from the same year found that nearly half of first- and second-year medical students believed that Black people had 'thicker skin' than white people, and that they felt less pain.[10]

On top of these injustices, this causes women to doubt their judgement and their bodies. We're inherently trained to believe that doctors know what they're doing and we should bow to their authority. Now, don't get me wrong. I'm not saying we should all be self-diagnosing on Google where, let's face it, regardless of the symptoms you put in, you'll be told you have some form of cancer. I think doctors are important and highly skilled, but they are fallible, and subject to the same unconscious biases and social narratives as the rest of us. You're not a hypochondriac or being difficult if you ask for a second (or even a third) opinion. God made our bodies so beautifully – I'm in awe of what they can do – which is why it's important to know, love and care for yours. That means fighting for it if necessary.

We can get into a cycle of gaslighting ourselves into thinking our pain can't be that bad. In 2022, Spain approved draft legislation proposing that workers who suffer from severe period pain should be entitled to between three and five days' medical leave per month, paid for by the state. This legislation hadn't passed at the time of writing, but if it does, Spain will be the first European country to provide a legal entitlement to menstrual leave.[11]

While there are many benefits to this system, particularly for employees who suffer from endometriosis or the painful effects of menopause, the primary fear among employers is that it will be open to abuse. But in reality, my experience is that no one wants to take time off for menstrual pain. For every woman who has deceitfully evoked 'women's problems' as a reason not to work, there will be a thousand who 'pushed through' when they really should have been working in bed with a hot water bottle on their stomachs. I don't want to keep using the tired comparison, but I can't imagine anything that caused 73% of men physical pain every twenty-eight days not being given extreme allowances to accommodate the inconvenience. Not every feminist thinks this is necessary though, as Germaine Greer announced in *The Female Eunuch*: 'Women are not more incapacitated than men are by their drinking habits, their hypertension, their ulcers and their virility fears. It is not necessary to give menstruation leave.'[12] My goodness, she must be a laugh at dinner parties.

So, what are we going to do about this? Here are some suggestions. First, if you're a medical professional, male or female, never use the term 'lady parts'. Second, be aware that this bias exists, whether in you personally or in the system as a whole, and do your best to observe and correct it when it crops up. Also – you're doing a great job and we appreciate you. For men – don't dismiss the women in your life when they say they're in pain. Take it seriously.

Whether or not it can be attributed to our 'lady parts' doesn't mean it's any less real or agonising. For women – the best advice my sister Cathie ever gave me was: 'When in the hospital, don't be a hero.' If doctors are likely to assume you're exaggerating your pain, and account for that in their treatment, you don't simultaneously want to be playing it down. Express your pain loudly, with enthusiasm and in no uncertain terms. Being a martyr will get you nothing but a place at the back of the queue.

The many identities of a woman

Tick all that apply

- ☐ Babe
- ☐ Ball and chain
- ☐ Ball-buster
- ☐ Bimbo
- ☐ Bitch
- ☐ Boss
- ☐ Bossy
- ☐ Bride
- ☐ Bridezilla
- ☐ Bubbly
- ☐ Career woman
- ☐ Catty
- ☐ Chatty
- ☐ Cheap
- ☐ Child
- ☐ Cold
- ☐ Cougar
- ☐ Curvy
- ☐ Darling
- ☐ Daughter
- ☐ Deceived
- ☐ Deceiver
- ☐ Demure
- ☐ Ditzy
- ☐ Diva
- ☐ Divorcee
- ☐ Easy
- ☐ Emotional
- ☐ Feisty
- ☐ Feminazi
- ☐ Feminist
- ☐ Fiancée
- ☐ Flirt
- ☐ Frigid
- ☐ Frumpy
- ☐ Girlfriend
- ☐ Girly girl
- ☐ Godly woman
- ☐ Good Christian girl
- ☐ Gossip
- ☐ Healer
- ☐ Heartbreaker
- ☐ Honey
- ☐ Hormonal
- ☐ Housewife
- ☐ Hysterical
- ☐ Ice queen
- ☐ Jailbait
- ☐ Kept woman
- ☐ Leader
- ☐ Loose
- ☐ Lover

The many identities of a woman

- ☐ Man-hater
- ☐ Mistress
- ☐ Modest
- ☐ Mompreneur
- ☐ Mother
- ☐ Mousey
- ☐ Mumsy
- ☐ Naggy
- ☐ Oversensitive
- ☐ Plus-size
- ☐ Preacher
- ☐ Prima donna
- ☐ Princess
- ☐ Prude
- ☐ Saint
- ☐ Sassy
- ☐ Seductress
- ☐ Shrew
- ☐ Shrill

- ☐ Sinner
- ☐ Siren
- ☐ Skinny
- ☐ Slag
- ☐ Slut
- ☐ Spinster
- ☐ Supermom
- ☐ Sweetheart
- ☐ Temptress
- ☐ Tomboy
- ☐ Trollop
- ☐ Trophy wife
- ☐ Villain
- ☐ Whore
- ☐ Widow
- ☐ Wife
- ☐ Working mother
- ☐ Yummy mummy

Don't call me baby

'What can I get you, sweetheart?'

'Sorry, what?'

'Anything to drink, darling?'

'Oh, erm, yes. Can I have a slimline tonic?'

'Sure, and anything for you, boss?' he said, turning to my male companion.

As I watched him scratch the drinks order onto his comically small waiter's pad, I felt a rage surging up inside me.

I surveyed the curtains of hair hanging over his forehead, popularised in the mid-nineties by the likes of Peter Andre and Nick Carter. I guessed they had made a comeback for the TikTok generation. He couldn't have been more than nineteen, yet this young man, brandishing a hairstyle that I remember from the last time round, had addressed me using terms I normally only hear from my mum. By contrast, the man next to me was his 'boss'. Far from overfamiliar, it was a mark of respect.

I wanted to stand up and shout at him that I was not his sweetheart, and my friend was definitely not his boss. And actually, if either of the two of us was qualified to be a front-of-house manager at a mediocre Harvester-imitation restaurant halfway between Slough and London, it would be me. It was either that or leave a strongly worded review on TripAdvisor. I calmed down and ended up doing neither – my rage never lasts long enough for me to document it online.

I want to be one of those jolly women who folds every waif and stray that prematurely uses a term of endearment towards them into their bosom and smothers them with love. But I'm not. There are few people I enjoy hearing pet names from: very close friends

43

(those I would call if I was crying), family and a romantic partner. That's the list. It doesn't include nineties-throwback-hairstyle-guy at fake Harvester. But it's not just when it happens to me that I get wound up.

When my sister was approaching her due date, she wanted to watch a show where it was guaranteed she wouldn't have to see any babies, pregnant women or childbirth. And so started our four-day *MasterChef* marathon. Greg Wallace (you know, the bald one) moved around the workstations with the magnanimity of a man who knew next week's lottery numbers. And he wouldn't stop referring to grown women as 'girls'. Go back and watch Series 12 for yourself if you don't believe me. But whatever you do, don't play one of those drinking games where you do a shot of tequila every time he says it. You'd end up in hospital on an IV drip. It got worse after a Black woman revealed that she worked as a surgeon on a children's ward, and, in a tone I only use when addressing the very cutest of puppies, he said: 'I bet your parents are proud, aren't they?' The very next person he spoke to, a white man, worked for the British Heart Foundation developing new treatments and preventative interventions, and I'm gutted to say we have no idea if his parents are proud. Greg didn't think to ask.

I can already hear the distant cries of: 'What *can* we say then?', so I'll tell you my preference. I like my name, and if you don't know it, I prefer to be referred to as a 'woman'. Not all women agree with me – some are very happy with 'lady' and others don't mind being a 'girl'. But I can't thumb-war everyone into submission. All I know is that 'babe', 'hun' and 'sugarplum' are off the table unless you know someone personally, and some adults feel patronised by 'girl' or even 'lady', as both carry behavioural implications. So play it safe and stick to 'woman'.

Bold as brass

Does every woman have to be a ho
Just because her job's unknown?

When I talk about drug addiction
And the cost of that affliction,
Do men have to message me
Asking if I paid on my knees?

Take the five victims of Jack the Ripper,
Is life worth less if you're a stripper?
Contrary to every newspaper report,
Only two of the five were escorts.

Mary Magdalene – woman of the night,
But have we even got that right?
Show me in the canonical text
Where it says she was paid for sex.
Pope Gregory the Great first made the declaration
In his sixth-century speech to the nation.
Since then we've assumed it was that way
And her influence has been downplayed.

So can we agree we won't any more
Assume any woman or girl is a whore?

Female competition – in search of world peace

If you've been in church circles you will have heard the phrase 'comparison is the thief of joy'. It's quoted so much that I had to check it wasn't actually from Proverbs and I'd missed David Suchet reading it to me on my last run of *Bible in One Year*. I found that it's actually credited to Theodore Roosevelt. In my life, comparison is no thief. Not because I don't indulge in it, but because you can't steal what is freely given. I'm very happy to hand over my joy in exchange for a decent compare-and-contrast session with another woman.

The comparison can take any number of forms, some of them genuine metrics of achievement and others just a bit pathetic. When I gave a TedX Talk, I forced myself not to check the views on the talks of other people who spoke on the same day, as I would only have been disappointed if I had fewer.

Then there are the women who end up dating the men I'm attracted to. I'll usually start by looking at the girth of their arms; I'd love to have a little less bingo wing. Then I look at their height, weight, hair, face, job and sense of humour. I like to know everything about the women whom men make me feel are better than me. I force myself to dissect my problems with the benefit of a more successful version of myself for comparison.

This all sounds a bit ridiculous, but I know it's not just me. And in a world of 'rear of the year' competitions and beauty pageants, who can blame us? Everyone else ranks women, so how are we supposed to rise above it?

Let's look at Liz Truss. Oh, don't pretend you've forgotten – forty-four days as the UK's prime minister, cruelly given a shelf life shorter than an iceberg lettuce. At the time, people said that her catastrophic tenure made Theresa May look good. But why were we comparing the two? Why not mention her predecessor, Boris Johnson? Because they were both Tory women running the country, they were put into their own category – away from the boys. I also heard some people say we couldn't have another female prime minister after Theresa May – as if her performance was linked in any way to another woman's. I've never heard anyone say that we couldn't have another male prime minister after Boris Johnson. Even though the logic is identical.

I wish I could say that the Church is immune to this kind of unfair comparison, but sadly Christian women probably feel it even more keenly. It doesn't help that the most celebrated woman in the Church was simultaneously a virgin *and* a mother. Sure, people will acknowledge that those not called to carry the Son of God would struggle to achieve the same, but it doesn't stop the pressure on women to achieve both perfect purity and godly motherhood. Sadly, the closest most of us will get to the Virgin Mary in this life is in a glass at a Sunday brunch when we're driving (or maybe on antibiotics or in recovery or preggers, or maybe we just don't fancy booze that day – there are lots of reasons people don't drink, okay? Get off my back).

I remember the first time I read Proverbs 31. (I think we all knew I was about to bring her up, and given that this is a note on comparison, it would be rude not to.) We read the passage in women's Bible studies, and she is pitched as someone to aspire to. The woman of Proverbs 31 feeds her family, makes their clothes and bedsheets by hand, makes money from trading, and works through the night. She gives to the poor, is wise, strong and faithful, and everyone in the community is well impressed by her. I remember following along, creating a mental tick list of the ways I was similar. Turned out there weren't many. I'm not her, but I've always harboured a sneaky suspicion that if I joined the Women's Institute, I could get there.

Regardless of my lofty dreams of knit-ins and bake sales, I think we all have to admit we're never going to be her. Proverbs 31 was the original 'have it all' woman, and it's unobtainable. I don't believe that in saying this I'm giving up or writing off God's vision for women. I believe we've missed the point.

Proverbs 31 is an acrostic: a piece of poetry where each line starts with the next letter of the alphabet. (Not in English, before you go and check, but in the original Hebrew.) In the Jewish tradition, it's the men who study this passage, learning it by heart. It was meant to have an audience of men, and was designed as an opportunity to praise and acknowledge women's achievements.

Old Testament scholar Ellen F. Davis explains that it's not there to lift up one individual superwoman, 'but rather to underscore the central significance of women's skilled work in a household-based economy'.[1] It's an ode to women, not an instruction to them. In *A Year of Biblical Womanhood*, Rachel Held Evans says: 'No longer presented as a song through which a man offers his wife praise, Proverbs 31 is presented as a task list through which a woman earns it.'[2] Ouch.

So, how can we pull this back? For a start, let's stop allowing our joy to be stolen… or handing it over. Let's not add fuel to the fire by googling people we think may be better than us. Let's all agree to lean more on God to help us stop feeling threatened by other people's achievements.

Let's not be those women who wear their inability to make female friends as a badge of honour. You know – the 'I just get on way better with men' ones. Women are not intimidating or a threat; they're on your side, and life is easier with a healthy mix of male and female friendships. Let's expect other women to be allies, and let's be allies ourselves. Let's be realistic about what we can achieve, and recognise that we all start the race from different places and will have different obstacles in our paths.

Ultimately, the only person we should be comparing ourselves to is Jesus; not the Virgin Mary or the woman of Proverbs 31. Just

Jesus. It's okay that we'll never measure up, but as we grow and get to know him better, we'll get closer.

Just in case that wasn't motivational enough for you, I've scoured the internet for the most toe-curling inspirational quotes on comparison. Picture the kind of stuff your Nana Mabel would have given you in a flowery card that had a ten-line poem in a cursive font on the cover. Okay cool, now you're ready:

'Don't compare your behind-the-scenes with someone else's highlight reel.'
Steven Furtick

'Personality begins where comparison leaves off. Be unique. Be memorable. Be confident. Be proud.'
Shannon L. Alder

'I'm too busy working on my own grass to notice that yours is greener.'
Unknown

'Admire other people's beauty and talent without questioning your own.'
Brooke Hampton

Oh yeah… and don't forget to live, laugh *and* love.

Lads lads lads

You may think that your hubby Hubert, son Simon or brother Bertie wouldn't have gone anywhere near any dodgy material when he was a teenager. No sir, it was all *VeggieTales* and the World Wide Message Tribe until he was eighteen years old. Well, I'm sorry to say that no teenage lad who isn't home-schooled and kept in a box avoids the clutches of misogynistic messages in the media. We all know sex sells, and unless someone's avoided advertisements all their life, they're probably way more interested in the sexy model than whatever product said 'babe' is selling. When I was young it was the lads' mags, stolen from someone's older brother and passed around the form room. I hate to say it, but the influences are almost certainly worse these days.

We all know that teenage boys can do and say some gross stuff. In my experience, *The Inbetweeners* is so accurate it's basically a documentary. But in the nineties, noughties and noughteens, lads' mags shaped the culture for boys, and as much as we would like to think our little angels were unaffected, their influence seeped into the lives of Christians too. Most people saw them as 'harmless banter'. I went on eBay and bought myself a couple of copies of the now-discontinued *Zoo*, *Nuts* and *FHM*, and had a little peruse with my cup of tea and Eccles cake. When it comes to having healthier conversations, it's important to acknowledge some of the influences that have shaped us. So, in the name of being as wise as serpents, I thought you should know what passed for acceptable chat when I was growing up, and what I would say to those comments now.

On women's looks: 'Please pass on the message that not all men like their ladies to put their slap on with a trowel' (Letters to the editor, *FHM* 2011).

Psst! Women can choose the make-up they like, rather than trying to please you, Mark from Swansea. Pass it on.

On speaking to your partner in the evenings, AKA 'vocal chloroform': 'Her stories [will be] about Geoff at work being a tyrant in meetings or her friend Kate's dilemma whether to cut her hair in a bob this summer' (*FHM* 2011).
Thankfully, the magazine was packed full of more interesting morsels for men to enjoy, like their article on how Theo Walcott looked like the fifth member of JLS.

On sex in marriage: 'If you put a penny in a jar every time you make love in the first year of marriage, and take a penny out every time you make love after that, the jar will never be emptied. Which is an odd coinage-related way of telling us that sex with the same person gets boring really fast' (*FHM* 2011).
This feels like a propaganda campaign for gonorrhoea.

On marriage: 'You'll both lose interest in seeing each other naked, but your "commitment" will mean you can't seek recourse in other, more nubile lovers' (*FHM* 2011).
Would it be easier if women just had a 'best before' date, a 'once opened consume within two months' disclaimer, so men will know the ideal time to discard us?

On funny women: 'I didn't realise a woman could have a man's sense of humour. It was an epiphany' (*FHM* 2011).
Yes, that coveted 'man's sense of humour' is one that all of us women strive for. I've been bingeing Lee Evans specials to see if I can get there.

On eating: 'Whereas [your mum] put in an 18-year shift producing you breakfast, dinner and tea, your girlfriend is much more likely

to have succumbed to the lure of the takeaway and the ready meal' (*FHM* 2011).
Maybe try praying 'Give us this day our daily bread' and see if Jesus comes up with anything?

On women's bodies: 'The sight of a bit of cellulite on the back of her legs fills you with existential depression' (*FHM* 2011).
You're in for a real treat when your wife gives birth, love.

On career development: 'We do live in a culture where foul-mannered a***holes seem to prosper, so you might as well join in and pull rank on anyone who's on a lower pay grade than you' (*FHM* 2011).
Oh good, just what the corporate world needs: another moron who's mean to the cleaning staff.

On Gary Lineker's new girlfriend: 'The former Tottenham hero is "besotted" with the 32C hottie' (*Zoo* 2007).
That's embarrassing, Zoo; there's a typo in her age. You accidentally slipped and added a 'C'.

On Alicia Silverstone's nude campaign for animal rights group Peta: 'Swap bacon for tofu for a glimpse of her body? For that, we need to see the, ahem, beef curtains' (*Zoo* 2007).
Lord, give me strength.

On being concerned about proposing: 'I would tie her to a sturdy chair, and not let her out of the room until she gave me the nod' (*FHM* 2001).
I've heard a lot of happy marriages start with a hostage situation.

Boys will *not* be boys

Heads up: this chapter contains some references to sexual violence towards women.

Boys will be boys

When I grew up, *American Pie* – the awkward coming-of-age film about a group of scamps who make a pact to lose their virginity on prom night – was huge. The task was simple: bag and bang a girl. Some did this by putting additional pressure on their existing girlfriend; some by taking up a hobby to snag a new girlfriend; others by lying about who they were or by getting girls drunk. They all watched and enjoyed porn, fantasised about lesbian relationships and, in one 'hilarious' caper, set up a hidden camera to watch a teenage girl get changed, only to accidentally broadcast it on the internet. What are boys like, eh?

It sounds unlikely now, but at the time I never heard anyone suggest this was problematic. Against a backdrop of noughties UK, it was hilarious and relatable. Boys wanted to get laid and they did whatever they could to achieve that goal, while it was the girls' job to hold out for as long as possible. The behaviours in the film were commonplace, laughed about and celebrated – particularly if they ended in sexual success.

When I first started writing this book, I felt so angry at the people who proliferated misinformation about what it was to be a man. The ones who felt 'men should be men', 'men are visual', 'they need a release', 'boys will be boys'. I was reading mainstream feminist manifestos and felt furious at the men who were encouraging other boys to walk down the same path. But

53

then I widened my reading. I read books by Christian women and then Christian men. I read challenges to mainstream and Christian feminism, and then I stopped feeling angry and just started feeling sad. I read *Take It Back* by Dr Tim Clinton and Max Davis. The cover has a picture of a man's arms held up in an X, fists clenched and veins throbbing.

The authors use imagery of boxers in the ring, armies and war. They speak of wilderness retreats and American football games and tool belts. They say men should be out in the wild in the mountains. They equate being manly with driving a pickup, flying a flag, riding a motorcycle, hunting, fishing, enjoying competition, shooting a gun or carrying a Bible. They warn Christian men against feminism and say: 'This solution does not work. Instead, it's destroying men. While the behaviour of some, not all, men is toxic, their masculinity is not.' They say 'traditional men' are being wiped out, and that liberals are trying to 'neuter' men.[1]

Then there's John Piper and Wayne Grudem's *Recovering Biblical Manhood & Womanhood*, which I quoted from earlier, specifying that masculinity is about the responsibility to lead women, and femininity is about affirming that masculinity and receiving that leadership. But some of the scenarios they use to illustrate how a man can do this in everyday life are truly bizarre. They ask how a man can carry a woman's purse while being masculine. They discuss what a postman should do to affirm his leadership as a man if he rings on a door and a woman answers. They discuss how a male lawyer can 'express his manhood' in a meeting of attorneys if that meeting has been called by a woman. And they talk about what to do if a man is driving and is lost, and there's no man around to ask for directions. How can he ask a woman without affecting his masculinity?

When I was speaking to people about this book, one person told me about a men's Christian conference that refused to offer a vegetarian option because 'real men eat meat'. During the first men's gathering at Mars Hill, a Seattle church founded by controversial pastor Mark Driscoll, each man was handed two rocks on entry and told, 'We're giving you your stones back.'[2]

You know what men are like...

This rhetoric isn't found just within the Church; controversial figure Jordan Peterson, who is regularly given mainstream platforms to speak about his extreme right-wing views on men and women, said: 'Men have to toughen up. Men demand it, and women want it, even though they may not approve of the harsh and contemptuous attitude that is part and parcel of the socially demanding process that fosters and then enforces that toughness.'[3] While language like this is damaging, it can't be accused of being hateful – and that's part of the problem. These widely accepted statements inch the acceptable discourse closer and closer to extremism. It affirms and encourages those who are at the more dangerous end of the spectrum to feel empowered. For example, extreme incel ideology – a hate movement where men who are 'involuntarily celibate' gather to share their experiences of women's rejection and the rights of men to sexual intercourse – is on the rise. This leads to horrific statements and actions, such as this comment on an incel forum: 'I wouldn't feel like a real man if I had consensual sex. Rape is the alpha method of pleasure and procreation.'[4]

What's scary is that these aren't isolated, crazy loners; there are people who have real influence within these extreme groups. One investigation found that a popular incel website was being run by Nathan Larson, a thirty-seven-year-old Virginia congressional candidate. He had written articles on father–daughter incest and petitioned for the Violence Against Women act to be repealed 'because we need to switch to a system that classifies women as property'.[5] Don't make the mistake of thinking this is just an American problem that doesn't exist in the UK. Watch Ben Zand's

Channel 4 documentary *The Secret World of Incels* if you want to hear from some on our side of the Atlantic.[6]

Don't get me wrong: the people mentioned above are not all the same. John Piper, Wayne Grudem, Dr Tim Clinton and Max Davis would, and do, stand firmly against this horrific ideology, and their position is designed to protect women in what they believe is a biblical way. Jordan Peterson isn't advocating for incels either, but I do believe that by widening the Overton window of acceptable mainstream discourse, he and others like him empower extremists to go one step further.

A real man?

As I said, I started off angry and then I just felt sad. I had this deflated feeling, as if I thought I was tackling a lion but when I went into the ring it was a small, scared tabby cat. I'm gutted that this 'masculinity' is so fragile that the postman needs to protect it when delivering packages to women. In *Recovering from Biblical Manhood & Womanhood*, Aimee Byrd says: 'Is God's created order that delicate, that a man needs to be careful about whether a woman giving him driving directions is doing it in a personal and directive manner?'[7]

Pushing boys and men towards this 'masculinity' is damaging for all of us. In their paper published in the *International Journal of Environmental Research and Public Health*, psychology academic Elisabeth Malonda-Vidal and her colleagues say: 'Traditional masculinity is characterized by instrumental personality traits such as aggression, self-affirmation, social dominance, and lack of consideration for others.'[8] In 2019, the American Psychological Association publicly acknowledged that 'traditional masculinity is psychologically harmful' and stressed the importance of encouraging men not to suppress their emotions.[9] Chimamanda Ngozi Adichie says: 'The harder you teach a man to be, the weaker his ego is. And then we do a much greater disservice to girls because we raise them to cater to the fragile egos of males.'[10]

One of the men in my Westlife focus group said that the need to understand what it is to be a man and to pursue 'manliness' can sometimes leave him feeling a little directionless in life. Another explained that, while he'd seen male headship modelled in his own family incredibly well, he felt it would be a huge pressure on him to take sole responsibility in leading his family. He said, 'There's been times in my life where I've actually spoken to my dad, and I've just said, "I don't think I can be that person. I'm not strong enough." I feel anxious about having to be the rock for everyone else. Because if there's a time when you're not feeling well, or a crisis happens, trying to be that person is impossible.' But his understanding of the realities and challenges of a marriage and family life is both attractive and desirable in a partner. When he gets married, that's what he'll have – a partner. Not an additional burden to carry, regardless of his own health and situation. He will have teamed up, so there will be two people to carry a collective burden, and when someone inevitably has to check out to recover from illness or deal with a crisis, the other is able to support them and keep going.

Dr Tim Clinton and Max Davis explain that real 'godly manhood' is following Nehemiah's example. The traits they associate with the prophet are: leading people in repentance; caring for the oppressed, enslaved and poor; feeding the hungry; redeeming slaves, and standing up for the weak. They explain that Nehemiah was 'fully immersed in his manhood'.[11] But I disagree. I would argue that these aren't things a *man* would do; these are things a *real follower of Christ* would do. There's nothing 'manly' about them; they are simply godly. They are for women to aspire to as well.

Putting the burden of world and family problems onto men's shoulders isn't fair or right; it cuts women out of the solutions and puts undue pressure on men. When I read through these descriptions and scenarios that illustrate 'godly masculinity', I struggle to see Jesus in them. Jesus was a man – he was wholly God and wholly man – so can't we look at his example? He didn't dominate, he didn't need to prove his masculinity, he wouldn't have been rocked by asking directions from a woman. Jesus is the wisdom of God, and in Proverbs 8 he's described using feminine language: 'Does not wisdom call out? Does not understanding raise her voice? At the highest point along the way, where the paths meet, she takes her stand' (Proverbs 8:1–2).

This doesn't affect Jesus' masculinity. In many ways he pushed against what his culture expected for manhood and exposed those roles as inadequate. He protected women and taught them as he did men, but he didn't feel obligated to provide for them financially and was happy for his ministry to be funded by women. He is the embodiment of the Spirit and displayed all of its fruits: love, joy, peace, patience, kindness, generosity, faithfulness, gentleness and self-control. He was the perfect man, and he didn't need women's affirmation or a hunting trip to prove it.

Our Mother who art in heaven

Stand up at your next elders/leadership/PCC meeting and say you feel passionately that going forward you should all start referring to God as 'our Mother', and with the pronouns she/her. I double dare you. Record the reaction and send it to me. I reckon the collective eye-roll would be enough to start a tsunami somewhere on the other side of the world. While you're at it, you could petition your local school to change 'history' to 'herstory', and see what happens.

If someone were to make this suggestion at my church, I can't tell you how much I would enjoy the drama. I would bring popcorn. But do I think we should refer to God as a woman? I don't. I'm not Ariana Grande. But do I think we could? Absolutely. God is no more male than he is female. Men *and* women were created in his image.

The reason for the male pronouns is obvious, given our history: we have to refer to God in some way, and history has dictated that authority is male. Plus, the fact is that Jesus ('Son' of God, not 'Daughter') referred to God as the Father and with male pronouns. And ideally we take our cues from him.

I can't imagine leaders of times gone by feeling comfortable worshipping a deity that defaulted to female pronouns. To be honest, I don't know if I would feel comfortable. This is almost certainly because of familiarity. It would feel odd to use gender-neutral or feminine language for God after years of he, his and him. And the women of All Saints agreed. One said that she always saw God as her Father and wouldn't be able to convert that image to a mother. The women of Sugababes felt it was all a bit too 'New Agey', but one of the men in Westlife said he was on board with anything that meant we said 'Daddy' less in church – and amen to that.

One of the women I spoke to was invited, as part of a group, to lead worship at a women's conference in the UK. When they got there, they were told that the conference leaders didn't want them to play any songs that referred to God as 'Father' because the husband of one of the women at the conference had a bad relationship with his dad, and she would feel triggered hearing it. She said, 'I couldn't believe that at a women's conference, a man was dictating how the women could worship.'

To me, the idea of praying to 'our Mother who art in heaven' seems like more of a political statement than a spiritual moment. It would feel awkward and clunky. But there is one example of God being portrayed as a woman that I have found deeply helpful, and that's in *The Shack*.[1]

In the 2017 film, God was played by Octavia Spencer – a Black woman. People found this shocking, expecting a Gandalf-like character with white wispy hair and a long beard (narrowing God to that image is probably best left to the makers of *The Simpsons*). I'd been a Christian for two years when I watched the film, and I really struggled with my idea of God and Jesus; I would have struggled with my view of the Holy Spirit too, but I hadn't even attempted to open that can of worms by then. I saw Jesus as a 'holier than thou' guy whose standards I could never live up to – which is sort of true, but not in the arrogant *Mean Girls* way I viewed him. I thought of God as harsh, his arm poised to smite me if I even glanced in the direction of debauchery. And then I watched *The Shack*, with a mother figure standing at the stove. All the wisdom, all the awesomeness, but with a new gentleness and kindness I hadn't considered.

God suddenly reminded me of the sage older women in my life, like my brother-in-law's mum, who always knows when I should stop working and go to bed, and comes straight off a night shift at a parole house to care for her grandchildren. Or my friend's Mexican mum who, after not sleeping for twenty-four hours because she was on an overnight flight from El Paso to London, stood in the kitchen and whipped everyone up a tortilla for lunch as a thank you for hosting her. I see God's love in these women, so why not see God depicted as them? We have to show him somehow, so to my mind it's as good a way as using a tall, ghostly seventy-year-old man.

But not everyone agrees. The film was described as 'heresy', 'a pretentious caricature', portraying God more as a 'New Agey Oprah Winfrey' than the God of the Bible, and Christians were called to be 'gravely concerned'.[2] God isn't a Black woman and no one watching the film would have walked away believing that. But as Chine McDonald points out, God as a Black woman is 'no more heretical than picturing him as a white man'.[3]

As one of the All Saints said, 'I know I've made God too small if I can't imagine him as anything more than a "he", but it's just what we've all learned. Also I wonder how many men would be comfortable with the idea of following an all-powerful mother.' One of the women in Sugababes disagreed, saying: 'We have to stop asking God to change. We are limiting him. Nothing we reinvent is going to be better than what he originally invented.'

We take our cues from Jesus, who referred to God as his Father, but Jesus also knew that God wasn't a man. God *is* a mother. In the Bible God constantly references himself (or herself – I don't even know any more!) as a woman. In *Theology of the Womb*, Christy Bauman lists numerous examples:[4]

- God as a mother eagle (Deuteronomy 32:11–12)
- God who gives birth (Deuteronomy 32:18; Job 38:29)
- God as a midwife (Psalm 22:8–10)
- God as mistress (Psalm 123:2–3)
- God as one who weans her child (Psalm 31:2)
- God as a mother hen (Matthew 23:37; Luke 13:34)
- God as a lioness (Ezekiel 19:2)
- God as a mother God (Hosea 11:3–4)

- God as a mother bear (Hosea 13:8)
- God as a conceiving and nursing mother (Numbers 11:12)
- God as a woman in labour (Isaiah 42:14)
- God as a nursing mother (Isaiah 49:15; 1 Thessalonians 2:7)
- God as a comforting mother (Isaiah 66:13)

Chine McDonald wrote an article for *Premier Christianity* in 2022, explaining why she was no longer using male pronouns for God: 'For me, this is about freeing God from the man-shaped box in which this male-dominated world has placed the creator.'[5] I believe if we had language that made it feel natural, and using non-male pronouns for God didn't feel like an extreme liberal statement, more people would do it. God is so much more than a man. If you, like me, are going to continue using male pronouns to describe him – let's agree that we will never lose sight of that.

Deal or no deal?

Bible babes

Next up on the Spiritual Shopping Channel we've got a really gorgeous gift set for any woman of the word. These stunning Bibles come in a wide range of colours – rose, fuchsia, blush and cherry blossom – and you can even pick your favourite of three messages to go on the cover: 'Beautiful Daughter of God', 'Jesus' Princess' or 'Feminine, Fun and Faith-filled'.

Each page is exquisitely laid out with a section at the bottom to explain the long words, and deep margins for all your fun doodles. This female version of the Bible includes a series of articles to help the modern woman, wife and mother to navigate challenges in a godly way. These include: emotional health, forgiveness, developing your gift of hospitality, running a cracking children's ministry, eating disorders and diet culture, performing your wifely duties, and how much make-up is too much?

We've even popped some handy bookmarks with a pretty flowery design into the key passages to save you time. Those are: Proverbs 31, much of Paul's teaching, and any mention of the Virgin Mary.

We are selling these stunning Bibles for just £15.99 while stocks last and, for a limited time only, we're throwing in a travel sewing kit embroidered with 'Sew on good soil' absolutely free!

Bible boys

But don't think it's just the girls who get all the fun – we've got gift Bibles for the men in your life too. Again, in a stunning collection of classic colours – tan, chestnut, coffee and sepia – these leather-bound Bibles are tough and durable, so they'll never let you down. You can choose one of three messages to have embossed on the cover of your gift Bible: 'Real Men Pray', 'Lead with Faith' or 'S†rong' (where the 'T' is replaced with a cross).

Inside, you'll find a clearly laid out and easy-to-navigate copy of the holy text, perfect for detailed study. There are helpful guides especially designed to challenge and develop your understanding of Scripture and push you forward in your mission for God. These include: finding your calling, triumphing over failure, bringing God into the workplace, taming the beast: men and their urges, showing compassion and mercy, men and physical health, leading even when you've not been asked to and how to challenge women on their outfits as a brother in Christ.

For an extra £10, each page will be laminated so you can take your Bible camping, fishing or mud wrestling without running the risk of it getting grubby. And, while stocks last, we will throw in a Bear Grylls pocketknife and a Yorkie bar completely free with every purchase. You can't say fairer than that.

Women aren't funny

CASSANDRA MARIA

Cassandra Maria is a comedian and presenter from Birmingham. She has performed stand-up in some of the UK's most famous comedy venues and presents a show on radio station Premier Gospel.

As a child I was never the funny one. I had five sisters and I went to an all-girls school. I was literally surrounded by women – and all of them were hilarious. I was better known as the weird one, the quiet one, the one who used to intentionally electrocute herself with the wire to her keyboard because the numb feeling was exhilarating on the tongue (don't try this at home, kids). It's a wonder I made it to working as a comedian.

I didn't care though. As a girl, being funny wasn't something you worked towards. It was only when I got to college and became more vocal with my thoughts that people started to think I had a funny bone after all. That's when I realised that, to the world, this made me an anomaly.

Fast-forward ten years and I found myself in the comedy industry as a creator, writer and performer. I had a few people say, 'You'll do great. You're a woman who's funny and you're attractive too. Honestly, you'll have no trouble!' This could not have been more incorrect. When I started out in comedy I immediately felt pitted against the other funny women in the industry. It was a blow to my self-esteem. It was as though there was only space for one funny woman on the whole of the internet. I'd often be accused of copying other female creators just because I was a woman telling jokes, even though their jokes were about wellies and mine were about tomatoes. It didn't matter to people. If you had a fanny and were funny you weren't allowed to co-exist.

Women are never allowed to be too many things. For example, if we're deemed attractive by the 'pretty gods', there are a lot of people who will resist finding us funny – you can't possibly be both things. But how is that fair? I once had a very well-known female comedian who was on at The Glee Club in Birmingham tell me I needed to 'disarm' the audience before cracking jokes. She said that as I was a woman, female audience members wouldn't be keen to laugh at my jokes and the men wouldn't want to laugh if they were with women, which they often were. Was I supposed to go out and tell everyone I'd let one rip just so they'd listen to me?! Couldn't I just go on, tell my jokes and leave without having to lay myself down on the altar of humility so as not to be threatening? It's not a problem I've seen men have to face.

I'll quickly clarify: I *love* the industry I'm in, and none of this has been a deterrent. It could sound like a 'woe is me' tale, but that's not what I'm getting at. I simply think it's important to flag up some of the issues I and other female comedians have on the circuit as a direct result of our sex.

In comedy, if you're an attractive woman, promoters will use your face to sell tickets. It's more demeaning than flattering. Once I had a promoter ask me to send a picture for his show's flyer. I sent him one where I wasn't dressed up to the nines, no make-up, just regular. He mistakenly sent me back a message meant for someone else, saying, 'I can't use this. She looks like a single mother with no job.' Erm, okay... so my talent and existing platform wasn't enough. I was there to offer eye candy. Being assessed on how hot you are doesn't do wonders for the old self-esteem.

If a woman does manage to make it through the 'don't be so attractive they see you as a threat, but be attractive enough to sell tickets' gauntlet, she then has the weighty responsibility of being funny – on behalf of all women everywhere. People will judge all women to be either funny or not funny based on her set alone. Post one joke that doesn't land on social media and she'll get comments like: 'This is why I don't watch any women comedians' or 'Women just aren't funny – they should stop trying'. The pressure of representing 50% of the global population with each gag doesn't create a light and breezy working environment. Do men carry the weight of all penises on their shoulders? Or are they allowed to represent themselves? I think you'll find it's the latter.

Then comes the final question, the biggie, the truth behind the Wizard's curtain, the reason everyone is playing Judge Judy over your every punchline: 'Are women even funny?'

Here's a conversation I've had a thousand times:

MAN: Hey. You're really funny.
ME: Aww, thank you!
MAN: It's rare to find a funny woman.
ME: Is it? I know lots of funny women.
MAN: No, honestly, it's a rarity. Women just aren't funny.
ME: Maybe they're just not funny to you?
MAN: Nah, they're not funny full stop. But that's why I like you – you're different, like you're actually funny.
ME: I feel sorry that you don't know more funny women.
MAN: All I need to know is you.

Aannddd doesn'treplyeveragain. Some men think this is a compliment and that by favourably comparing me to my sisters they make themselves more appealing to me. In fact, it does the opposite. If you, as a man, have *never* met a funny woman in your life, I'm afraid you don't speak to women other than when you're paying a female cashier in Tesco. Or, even worse, you don't see women as individual humans and therefore have never considered that they could be funny.

To answer the pertinent question: yes, women are *very* funny. I'll be honest, there may not be as many funny women as there are men, simply because we were never encouraged to develop that skill. Men are pushed to be funny, charming and sexy, whereas women are encouraged to be sweet, classy and beautiful. That's why women are intimidated by the most beautiful woman in a room and men by the funniest. Women's humour is often overlooked because we live in a world where men have already ordained themselves hilarious. The humour barometer is set by men who are convinced that they are the arbiters of hilarity. But women have their own brand of humour and it's just as strong as men's.

I've had hundreds of women say to me over the years, 'I'd love to do what you do. I think I'm hilarious. I just don't have the confidence.' How sad is that? Women have a unique perspective on the world; our view, our commentary *and* our comedy are needed. If you think you have that gift of making people laugh, you should absolutely be able to explore it without being scrutinised extra harshly because of your sex.

Comedy is empowering. Exploring your own brand of humour takes guts, even if it's just telling jokes to a friend or at a dinner party. It requires bravery, as it goes against the expectations the world puts on women. So please, women, get out of the kitchen (unless you've chosen to be there – after all, a girl's got to eat) and explore all of your quirks, humour and weirdness. Be funny and fierce in a world that says you must only be pretty and polite. Have confidence in *you*.

A biblical girl's guide to...

If churchgoing women are meant to be passive and unassuming, then biblical women didn't get the memo. Let's explore the very particular set of skills acquired by these remarkable women.

Camping with Jael (Judges 4:16–24)

But Jael, Heber's wife, picked up a tent peg and a hammer and went quietly to him while he lay fast asleep, exhausted. She drove the peg through his temple into the ground, and he died.
(4:21)

Camping can be uncomfortable at the best of times; anyone who's been to a Christian festival will tell you that. But if you can get over the questionable shower block and waking up in the night because your nose is so frozen you're not sure it's still there, there's a lot to be said for a brief dalliance with a nomadic lifestyle.

The key is to make sure your tent is so firmly pitched it'll never blow away – and that's all in the tent pegs. You've really got to drive those puppies right the way down into the ground. Make sure they're firmly in there. I also keep a few spare, just in case I find there are some structural issues, or another tribe's leader needs sorting out.

Gardening with Eve (Genesis 2:4 – 3:24)

Adam named his wife Eve, because she would become the mother of all the living.
(3:20)

I blooming love a garden – pun intended. When designing your perfect outdoor space, I recommend a river flowing through the middle – it'll save you a lot of time watering. Plus, I like to have a big tree as a central focal point.

The garden is a great source of food, although do be careful about what you choose to eat. You can get into a right pickle if you go scrumping on the wrong tree. Your greenery is also an adequate material for fashionable undergarments. Of course, everyone knows I favour a fig leaf, but don't feel restricted – as long as you get decent coverage of the essentials, that's all that counts.

Childbirth with Shiphrah and Puah (Exodus 1:15–21)

The midwives, however, feared God and did not do what the king of Egypt had told them to do; they let the boys live. (1:17)

Thanks to our lovely gardening expert, childbirth can be quite a challenge for women. We adhere to all the old classics: the deep breathing, the squeezing of a hand, the swearing never to let our husbands come near us again as long as we live. Although in our day they were nowhere near to hear these emphatic vows.

When it comes to the delivery room, the fewer people the better. Don't let all those cooks spoil the broth. Sometimes you'll be given instructions that don't feel right to you, and this is where your experience, intuition and faith come into play. Do this well and follow God's commands over those of the world, and you could go down in history.

Stripping with Vashti (Esther 1)

For the queen's conduct will become known to all the women, and so they will despise their husbands and say, 'King Xerxes

commanded Queen Vashti to be brought before him, but she would not come.'
(1:17)

My rule of thumb when it comes to stripping – or any public display of the intimate parts of my body – is that it's best not to. Now, I could tell you which perfumes to bathe in and what jewellery to adorn yourself with for the public art of seduction, but I would rather just stay in my chambers wearing all my clothes. This may anger some people – husbands, kings and so on – who want to display their assets by showing off yours. But in my experience, it's better to disappoint a king than to disappoint yourself.

This may result in the ending of a relationship, but good riddance to anyone who tried to pimp you out, I say. You're better off out of it. Never be afraid to stand your ground. Many people know that the defiance of a woman appearing in front of the king can change the course of history. But I managed to change the course of history by refusing to.

Translating with Huldah (2 Kings 22:14–20)

She said to them, 'This is what the LORD, the God of Israel, says: Tell the man who sent you to me, "This is what the LORD says: I am going to bring disaster on this place and its people, according to everything written in the book the king of Judah has read."'
(22:15–16)

Sometimes even the best of us need help working out exactly what someone is saying. When Google Translate or Netflix subtitles won't do the job, powerful people have to call in a professional. I speak 'God'. I know it's not technically a language, but to be honest we all need a bit of help understanding his meaning from time to time.

When righteous kings seek me out to shed some light on a murky situation, I'm more than happy to oblige. My main advice is not to mince your words. If you know what God is saying, don't be embarrassed to let them have it, full force. No sugarcoating required. Sometimes God reads people the riot act – and if you're called to play your part, play it well.

Women in church leadership: heroes or heretics?

I grew up in a church led by a single female Baptist minister. As a child you don't question the theological robustness of that decision. You just rock up, eat the raisins your mum gives you to keep you quiet, and pray for the sweet reprieve of Sunday school. This minister was, and is, wonderful. No leader is perfect, but I've now been part of a number of churches, and I've never seen anyone immerse themselves in their community and invest so much in individuals and families as she does. She is universally loved.

I'm not using an anecdote of one incredible woman as justification for women in leadership. But it does frame my approach to the topic. It was only when I came back to the Church aged twenty-five, and was part of a congregation that wouldn't have allowed a female primary, that I realised it was even up for discussion.

There are many churches where women are not allowed to lead, lots where they aren't invited to speak from the front, some where they're not even permitted to preach to the children, and a handful where they're forbidden to speak during Bible studies. Some people believe that supporting women in ministry is a slippery slope leading to liberalism and agnosticism. I even read one suggestion that having female preachers could lead to bestiality. I struggle to see the link but, for some people, female preachers are just another step down the path to a Bunga Bunga party.

Beth Allison Barr is a professor and expert in Medieval and Early Modern England and Church History. She tells a story of a theologically conservative male student who expressed concern about her choice to continue teaching as a wife and mother. In one of her lectures, he suggested in all seriousness that she clear her teaching material with her husband before presenting it to the classroom.[1]

During an absolutely fascinating conflab with two of the sisters of the Community of Our Lady of Walsingham, the committed Catholics explained that they didn't aspire to be priests and agreed that it was a role for men. But they were clear that there were other positions of leadership and influence in the Church where women must be represented in order to serve the congregation and community well.

Conflict

Everyone knows there's conflict around the idea of female vicars; just look at the response Geraldine Granger got when she rocked up at Dibley. This is a debate that divides churches and church groups, and is discussed in most denominations including, for a minority, the Catholic Church. Mary McAleese, a Catholic and former Irish president who was voted sixty-fourth most powerful woman in the world by *Forbes* magazine in 2005,[2] has spoken out on the issue. In an interview with Mary Ann Sieghart, author of *The Authority Gap*, she said:

The exclusion of women in my Church greatly bothers me. Because it represents 1.2 billion people, one in six people in the world, I feel I can't walk away. My own Church is an empire of misogyny. It has carried down the 2000-year conduit attitudes that are still embedded in societies all over the world.[3]

While evangelical Christian theologian Kat Armas says:

The first time I was called a heretic was for believing that women could preach, a belief based on my in-depth study of the biblical text. I wasn't called a heretic because I denied the Trinity, the resurrection, or any of the core tenets of Christianity. Perhaps so many young people are fleeing from the church because of these dichotomous, 'all or nothing' views of faith that disregard life's complexities.[4]

Despite the Church of England allowing women to be ordained since 1992 and to be bishops since 2014, there is still some resistance to the idea. As previously mentioned, 430 members of the clergy resigned from their positions in the Church of England after a motion was passed to allow the ordination of women. And men can still choose not to be ordained by a male bishop if they know that the bishop has previously ordained women.

Reverend Lucy Winkett tells how she was celebrating mass at St Paul's Cathedral when a confused visitor asked a verger, 'Why is that priest speaking with a woman's voice?'. And Bishop of London, Dame Sarah Mullally, says, 'Since I've been a bishop, I've been very much more conscious of my gender. I stand at the back of the church and as people leave they will say things like, "Oh, I didn't know what to expect from a woman, but you were all right," or, "You're actually quite pretty really".'[5]

There are many biblical references made by both camps on this issue. Stephen Parkinson of Forward in Faith, an international pressure group opposed to women priests, says, 'Jesus chose 12 men, he did not choose women. He cocked a snook at every convention. If he'd wanted women priests, he'd have had them. If he is God incarnate, then he should know.'[6] But others disagree, as he's known to have discipled women, including Mary Magdalene, Joanna and Susanna, who accompanied him in his ministry and supported him (Luke 8:1–3). Many believe that Jesus' radical welcome towards these female apostles is a sign of his progressive attitude towards women in leadership.

The early Church was packed full of women, including Junia, who was not only an apostle but was prominent among the apostles.

Throughout history, people have changed the name to Junias (a male name), considering it unlikely that she was a woman, given her position, and some Bible translations only restored her to Junia in 1998. But she's not the only prominent woman in the early Church; in Romans 16 Paul honours ten women – Phoebe, Priscilla, Mary, Junia, Tryphena, Tryphosa, Persis, Rufus's mother, Julia and the sister of Nerus – and seventeen men, who were part of the first group to share the gospel. Given that he allowed such honour and prominence to women who led in the early Church, why do many believe Paul didn't support female leadership?

Paul on women – less chat, more hat?

There are two passages that cause conflict when it comes to women leading in church, and both were written by Paul. In 1 Corinthians 14:34–35, he says:

> Women should remain silent in the churches. They are not allowed to speak, but must be in submission, as the law says. If they want to inquire about something, they should ask their own husbands at home; for it is disgraceful for a woman to speak in the church.

Given that the rest of 1 Corinthians 14 is concerned with speaking in tongues, some believe that Paul was specifically talking about women speaking in tongues in church. But I remember very early on in my faith journey my conservative Ukrainian Bible group leader explaining her understanding of these verses. She said that, at the time, the gatherings would have been packed full; men would stand at the front near the speaker and women would stand at the back. There was no sound system or microphone, so it was unlikely that the women would have been able to hear the person speaking at the front, so they did what most of us who are gathered in a crowd unable to get involved in the action would do: they had a chinwag. Of course, this made it more difficult for the men to hear what was going on and inhibited the teaching, so Paul instructed the women to stop chatting.

The second passage is in Paul's first letter to Timothy: 'I do not permit a woman to teach or to assume authority over a man; she must be quiet. For Adam was formed first, then Eve' (1 Timothy 2:12–13).

According to Junia Project's Gail Wallace, the word Paul used for 'authority' when he was writing in Greek was *authentein*, but the English translation has limitations. The word only appears in the Bible once, and only rarely in extra-biblical texts – but when it does crop up it's associated with aggression. *Authentein* is translated as 'domineer' in the Latin. In the rest of his writing, Paul uses the word *exousia* to refer to authority. Gail Wallace adds, 'Using this passage to restrict women in leadership requires elevating a handful of verses over the rest of Paul's writing, not to mention the entire New Testament.'[7]

Theologian Dr Sandra Richter agrees. In a lecture she gave at Asbury Theological Seminary in 2015 (yes, that's the same place as the 2023 revival), she explained that if these verses are to be taken at face value, Paul greatly contradicts himself. Earlier in his Corinth letter he advises women to cover their heads when they prophesy in church. This instruction is surely redundant if women aren't to open their mouths in church at all. He talks about his fellow workers in Christ, Priscilla and Aquila – a married couple who run a house church. In this patriarchal society, men were always named first unless the woman was of a higher class. But nowhere in Paul's writings does he pay even a moment's attention to status. It's far more likely that Priscilla is named first because she's recognised as the more influential speaker, a prominent preacher and further to the forefront of the movement.[8]

The overall message that Paul promotes is one of unity. In Galatians 3:28 he says: 'There is neither Jew nor Gentile, neither slave nor free, nor is there male and female, for you are all one in Christ Jesus.' Distinguished New Testament professor Beverly Roberts Gaventa explains that we have missed Paul's wider purpose in our reading of these passages. Where he asked for oneness, we have imposed controlling borders for uniformity. She says we are invited to 'think along *with* Paul' (emphasis mine), rather than to weaponise his words against women.[9]

The fact is, Paul *did* let women speak; he didn't want them to be silent. He didn't expect that of the women around him. Beth Allison Barr says, '[Paul] allows women to speak throughout his letters (1 Corinthians 11:1–6 is a case in point). Paul is not limiting women's leadership; he tells us with his own hand that women lead in the early church and that he supports their ministries.'[10]

In her book *The Moment of Lift*, Melinda Gates says, 'Disrespect for women grows when religions are dominated by men.'[11] Whether or not the Church hands women the mic or gives them a title, they will teach and preach and share the gospel. I'm surrounded by wise women who guide me with their deep knowledge of the Bible. Kat Armas says, 'Many of us have or know a strong, devoted unrecognised theologian who has served as a madre of our faith. A deacon of light on our spiritual journey.'[12]

Opposers of this view will sometimes say that when women teach or preach in the Bible, God is making a point that there were no good men to stand up and take the reins at the time. Aimee Byrd says, 'This argument never holds traction, as we all know God can use Balaam's ass (Num. 22:21–41) if he chooses. He can raise up men, women, and donkeys to carry out his Word. He doesn't need the so-called important people.'[13] I truly believe that if we see a woman doing something great in the Bible it is by God's deliberate choice, not a plan B.

On a practical rather than a biblical note, speaking to members of my former female-led church, one pointed out that when the reverend left and was replaced with a man, the men began attending the church again. One of the All Saints, who is training for ministry herself, said, 'I am afraid that I'll just become leader of a weird women's church that isn't at all diverse. A man might say he would follow a woman, but in reality wouldn't he really prefer a Pete Hughes?' (Disclaimer: other excellent male church leaders are available.)

This is worth bearing in mind, but definitely shouldn't mean women can't lead churches. It's just that they should be aware this dynamic exists and make sure men are visible from the front too – just as I believe a man should have visible women at the front of any church he is leading.

Jesus versus the times

The times

The female line was of no importance, with all priority placed on the patriarchal lineage.

Jesus...

acknowledged the women in his lineage – not just the celebrated ancestral mothers, but immigrant non-Israelite women too: widowed and abandoned Tamar, the presumed prostitute Rahab, Ruth the Moabite, and the wife of Uriah, known as Bathsheba, the woman King David sexually assaulted in 2 Samuel 11.

(See Matthew 1:1–17.)

The times

The testimony of women was not to be believed; only men could be competent witnesses. A woman's place was in her home and not in court. If women came forward with a credible-sounding testimony, it was acceptable practice to pay guards to say that the women were lying.

Jesus...

waited until Mary and Mary Magdalene came to the tomb, and revealed himself to them. He instructed women to share what they'd witnessed with others, including men. He gave women the honour of testifying to the single-most significant moment in history.

(See John 20:11–18.)

The times

Women were of inferior intellect and not worth educating. They received minimal education and were taught housework and embroidery. Most women didn't have a good grasp on the spoken Hebrew language, let alone reading and writing.

Jesus...

affirmed Mary for sitting with his male followers and listening to him teach, saying that she had 'chosen what is better' compared to the housework that was expected of her.

(See Luke 10:38–42.)

The times

Women were supposed to be quiet, never questioning what they were told by a man.

Jesus...

allowed women to petition him with requests. He freed them to press in to the kingdom of God and showed them grace and mercy when they were in a place of great pain.

(See Matthew 15:21–28.)

The times

Rabbis didn't speak to women in public, even their own wives, especially women at wells, as it was a local pickup spot. Any woman, any Samaritan and anyone of ill repute was to be despised.

Jesus...

spoke to and asked favours of a Samaritan woman who was an outcast. He took an interest in the intimate details of her life and encouraged her to live better.

(See John 4:1–26.)

The times

Women who had sinned were dirty; they were not allowed anywhere near others and certainly weren't allowed to touch them.

Jesus...

elevated a woman who was known to be 'a sinner', allowed her close

contact with him and used her as an example to teach a religious leader a lesson.
(See Luke 7:36–50.)

The times
Women were ideally not to be seen out in public. If they had to leave the house, they always had to be escorted by an appropriate male. They weren't encouraged to follow religious leaders.
Jesus...
encouraged female followers to join him, accompany him during his ministry and financially support his work.
(See Luke 8:1–3.)

The times
A woman who was bleeding was seen as ceremonially and socially unclean, and was to be ostracised. If she touched anyone she would impart her uncleanness to them, meaning they couldn't take part in any aspect of Israel's worship. Therefore, she should be too embarrassed to be out in public.
Jesus...
shared his power with women. He didn't make a woman feel ashamed for drawing close to him in faith. He showed tenderness and kindness to a woman in deep distress, and when society said she couldn't touch him, he affirmed and blessed her for doing so anyway.
(See Luke 8:44–48.)

The times
A woman caught cheating was worth nothing. You could parade her around in public, shame her and ultimately kill her by stoning. A woman was to be treated more harshly than a man who had committed the same crime.
Jesus...

refused to judge a woman's sin more harshly than the sin of any other. He responded with gentleness and compassion in the face of the woman's shame. He didn't take her life away; he offered her the opportunity of a new one.

(See John 8:1–11.)

Don't whistle while we work

In life, we struggle to trust women

I was once on holiday with some friends, and we were talking about popular myths that people believe, but aren't true. You know the ones – like how humans only use 10% of their brains, or you should pee on a jellyfish sting, or Jesus was white. I contributed my fact, which was that, while the theory is correct, in practice it's not actually the case that water goes down the plughole in a different direction depending on the hemisphere you're in. The three blokes around the table explained that I was wrong. One of them had crossed the hemisphere while travelling and had recorded the phenomenon in action. I said that I had been surprised too, but I had taken the time to research it and discovered that the direction is down to the position of the tap and the dimensions of the basin. I suggested the dimensions had been different in the two basins he had tested the theory on. Uproar ensued and I was dismissed by the group, who adamantly defended their position. We didn't have internet access at the time, so much like with all pre-2010 pub disputes, we had to leave it there.

Later in the trip, when we had been able to access Google, one of the guys checked my facts, verified I was correct and never brought it up again. This was a particularly boysie holiday and the blokes definitely hyped each other up. I reckon that speaking to them individually I would have been given more credit for my research ability – I didn't get my neuroscience degree from a cracker. But collectively I was shouted down and it felt awful.

It may sound like a silly incident, but this kind of thing happens more often than is comfortable. *The Authority Gap*'s Mary Ann

Sieghart highlighted the trivial annoyance of realising her husband independently checked facts she knew to be true.[1] In 2020, journalist Eileen Mary tweeted: 'Thinking about the time I said that I was distantly related to Marie Curie and a guy explained "It's pronounced Mariah Carey".'[2] And then there was the time scientist Jessica McCarty was challenged at a NASA Earth meeting: 'A white male post doc interrupted me to tell me that I didn't understand human drivers of fire, that I def needed to read McCarty et al.' In response she looked him in the eye, pulled her hair off her name badge and said: 'I'm McCarty et al.'[3]

There's been much discussion about this experience where men will override a woman's expertise with their own confidence. The term 'mansplaining' was coined by Rebecca Solnit in her book *Men Explain Things to Me*,[4] giving new vocabulary to every woman who has been offered unsolicited advice about their gym technique from a male stranger. I once told a friend that he was mansplaining something to me, but he immediately stopped me and told me I obviously didn't know the definition of mansplaining, before correcting me. I pointed out the irony, but he still didn't find it funny. I've also heard the phenomenon described as 'correctile dysfunction'.

This is all very funny, and the tweets bring us many a collective laugh around the dinner table, but there are examples when the stakes are high and the consequences dire. In one study, participants were divided into small groups. Each group was given information about a family and asked to make a theoretical custody decision based on what they had been told. Information was given to one member of the group, who then shared it with the rest of the group before deliberating. The researchers found that information was six times more likely to be paid attention to and included in the decision-making process if it were conveyed by a man. What does this indicate about juries when they're deliberating cases, and the weight they give different people's testimony? It's deeply concerning.

In 2016, a clip of a Black female doctor went viral when she shared her experience of trying to help an unwell passenger on a plane. Dr Tamika Cross explained that she was prevented from attending to the sick person because the cabin crew didn't believe she was a medic. She was told, 'Oh no, sweetie. Put ur hand down; we are looking for actual physicians or nurses or some type of medical personnel. We don't have time to talk to you.'[5]

Sadly, this is an area where race plays an undeniable role in making the situation harder for women of colour. Kat Armas says: 'Reports show that ethnic as well as gender bias are a common phenomenon among health-care professionals. These biases increase two- and even threefold among Black people – especially women.'[6] But it's not just in healthcare. When Dawn Butler, a Black Labour MP, first went into the House of Commons, she got into the lift only to be told, 'This lift really isn't for cleaners,' by another Member of Parliament.

In a study, subjects were asked to listen to a conversation and then recall what had been said. Participants were more likely to make mistakes when repeating remarks made by Black women than those made by white women, Black men or white men.

A Black male friend told me he had sat in on a meeting at a major investment bank where one of the more junior employees – a Black woman – was told she would be going off site for a meeting the following day. She was given advance notice by a white female colleague that it would be formal, so she shouldn't wear any short shorts, and that there would be security and metal detectors, so she shouldn't 'bring any knives or anything like that'. Both he and the junior employee reported the comments, but no formal action was taken.

One of the women in the All Saints focus group, again a woman of colour, shared a story from when she was working for a charity as part of their legal team, a job that required her to have a law degree and sign a universal non-disclosure agreement. She told how her male line manager was presenting in a meeting when he stopped and turned to her, addressed her by name, and said, 'I guess this is for you. I just need to clarify that none of this should leave the room.' As if she was taking notes ready for a girly gossip over paninis at lunch. Give me strength.

These are just some of the many jaw-dropping stories that are all too common for women, and especially women of colour. The systematic underestimation, infantilising and patronising has to stop. It's hard enough for women to be offered high-powered jobs, but once they do get into them, many just want to break out again and be in a space where they're respected and shown value. Who would want to be the woman who has to prove, bit by bit, day by day, on behalf of her entire race and gender, that she knows not to wear batty riders to a corporate business meeting? Dispelling stupid stereotypes like that is a full-time job in itself – let alone doing, and feeling the pressure to excel at, your actual job.

Women in charge

People find it hard to take instructions from women. Back in the eighties, my mum and dad were doing up their home. They didn't have much money, so did a lot of the work themselves. My mum rewired our semi-detached house using a book on electrics – there were no YouTube tutorials back then. When it came to building projects, she really knew what she was doing. At one point they had builders doing some work to the outside of the property. Dad wasn't around, so Mum was overseeing everything, and she saw a man making a mess of the pointing on the side of the house. She went to the foreman and said that this man wasn't doing a good job. He laughed and said, 'Oh yeah? What type of pointing do you want him to do then?' She politely explained that because of the rainfall she wanted weathered pointing. The next day a new builder was working on it and it looked great. It turned out the actual pointer hadn't turned up the day before, so they'd asked the van driver to slap some cement between the bricks, thinking she wouldn't know the difference. Take a bow, Mum. Take a bow.

I had a similar, but less satisfying, moment when I was redoing my bedroom and I stripped the wallpaper with my handyman mate Charlie. Half the plaster came off with it, so we had to get plasterers in to take it all out, put up fresh plasterboard in places and replaster the room. They came one morning and started work, while I nipped out to buy paint samples and Charlie worked on something in the other room. When I came back, they hadn't put up the plasterboard we'd agreed. When I challenged the plasterer, he told me: 'Don't worry, love. I've explained it all to your boyfriend.' I can confirm that I *was* worried and had multiple follow-up questions.

Women find it hard to be respected as bosses. Of the UK's 100 biggest listed companies, only six currently have female CEOs.[7] The gender gap at the top is likely to close, however, and one of the guys in the Westlife focus group, who works in finance, made a great point. He said that in his company there are roughly equal numbers of men and women among the employees who are thirty-five and under. But for the jobs that require more experience, the qualified pool of women isn't big enough for equal representation – *yet*. But now that the junior and mid-level roles are full of women, they will hopefully continue to progress and take a larger share of those senior jobs in the future.

Psychologist Tomas Chamorro-Premuzic explains what he believes to be the problem when it comes to listening to women: 'Because we (people in general) commonly misinterpret displays of confidence as a sign of competence, we are fooled into believing that men are better leaders than women.'[8]

This is a problem in itself, but it weighs even more heavily on women, as ironically they are also penalised for showing confidence, while men aren't. Mary Ann Sieghart says, 'Researchers in Australia found that women do ask for a pay rise just as often as men. They are just not given it. Women are often punished for being as assertive as men.' She suggests that this is because women, unlike men, are rewarded for being likeable. People expect to see a woman's warmth and passion. This gives women a whole additional scale on which to be assessed that men don't need to concern themselves with.

I was recently criticised by a friend. He'd asked if I was nervous before a talk I was scheduled to give and I'd told him no, because I was prepared and I was good at public speaking. My certainty in my own ability was interpreted as arrogance. But he'd asked me about something that is specifically my job. Would you judge a medical consultant for saying she wasn't nervous ahead of an operation because she was well-practised and skilled in that area? If anything, you'd be relieved. Anything that requires expertise is nerve-wracking to someone who doesn't have that expertise. If my friend had asked me to remove an appendix, he would have seen a far less self-assured version of me.

Dangerous women

A YouGov poll conducted in 2016 for the Trades Union Congress and Everyday Sexism Project found that more than half of all women and almost two-thirds of young women have experienced sexual harassment in the workplace.[9] The majority – 80% – said they didn't report this for fear it would affect their career and they wouldn't be believed. Of the 20% who did report it, three-quarters said nothing changed and a sixth said they were treated worse afterwards.

As if that isn't enough of an injustice, men are now avoiding women for fear of being accused of sexual assault. In Texas, a female communications consultant was told by a male superior that they had to stop having meetings over lunch. He said, 'I've been told it's not appropriate for a married man to have lunch with a single lady.'

He even considered moving her to a different team to avoid any chance of giving the wrong impression.

Former Vice-President of the United States Mike Pence told journalists that he would never eat a meal alone with a woman who wasn't his wife. Activist Laura Bates says: '[The Pence Rule] was celebrated by some but it could have a massively detrimental impact on women's career trajectories in a fast-moving political world in which meeting over meals is common.'[10] A study at the University of Houston found that 27% of men avoid one-on-one meetings with female colleagues, and 21% are reluctant to hire women for jobs involving close interpersonal interaction with men, for example roles that involve travel.

There is a culture of putting boundaries in place between men and women in the Church, and – depending on what those are – I don't think it's a bad thing at all. For example, if I'm praying for a man, I always rope in a third person to pray with us. Prayer is spiritually intimate and I like the additional support. But in a professional setting, I don't see any reason to avoid a business lunch. We're not talking candlelight and four courses. We're talking a lunch in the daytime where you can mutually exchange ideas and strategy. It only becomes improper if you make it improper. Laura Bates says: 'Not one of these men seems to have considered that they could have achieved the same effect by simply not sexually harassing or assaulting any women.'[11]

A lot of this, of course, comes down to a fear that these women will make false accusations – something I'll cover at length in an upcoming chapter. Laura Bates points out that making men afraid of women is dangerous, particularly to the most vulnerable among us. Suggesting that this issue is about individuals rather than a much broader social construct means that the heart of the matter is never addressed, which negatively impacts the safety and rights of women across the globe.[12]

Everyone wins with more women

There are perks to female leadership. Research from the BI Norwegian Business School suggests that, on average, women score more highly on all five traits for leadership: agreeableness, extroversion, openness to new experiences, emotional stability and conscientiousness.[13] And in 2018, research from a Boston consulting group found that, on average, female-led businesses receive half the investment levels of male-led businesses, but generate twice the revenue.[14]

According to Mary Ann Sieghart in *The Authority Gap*, research shows that, statistically, houses listed by female estate agents sell for higher prices, female lawyers are less likely to behave unethically, and patients treated by female doctors are less likely to die or be readmitted to hospital. Female politicians do more constituency work than men, are less corrupt and have a leadership style that is more co-operative and inclusive. Countries that have more women in power are less likely to go to war and are less likely to have a civil war. Meanwhile, including women in peace processes makes them more successful and long-lasting.

There could be many reasons for these findings. A 2010 academic study on group intelligence found that collective intelligence was positively correlated to the proportion of women. The groups with one woman performed better than all-male groups, and group intelligence was more strongly correlated to gender diversity than to the IQs of the individual team members.[15]

Katherine Phillips, a professor of business and organisation, conducted an experiment where she put people in groups to investigate a murder.[16] In some groups all participants knew each other, but these groups performed less well than groups that included an 'outsider'. This is because the groups with less familiarity thought harder about the problem. The group with the least diversity was also more confident about its final answer, even though it was more likely to be wrong. What does this show us? That it may be more comfortable to be in a homogenous group, but it's not as effective.

Love, honour and no way

Weddings

When it comes to my friends' nuptials, I never see their wedding style coming. One of my mates isn't wearing white; she's opting for a suit in a colour she refuses to disclose to me. Another, who is very happy to take on the lion's share of the housework, has insisted on keeping her own last name. While some would be absolutely mortified if their partner asked their dad's permission before proposing, others would call the whole thing off if he didn't. So, who's right and who's wrong?

Look, I'm not married, but my first job was as an assistant to the woman who set up Virgin Brides for Richard Branson, and I can tell you, the couples who have the best weddings are the ones who don't sweat the small stuff. I had one bride lock herself in a toilet cubicle because there was a protest going past the central London reception venue and she was worried her guests wouldn't be able to hear the string quartet over the noble cause of the troops outside. But I've also had a bride who was desperate to go into the ceremony venue before the service started because her Iranian relatives were dancing in the aisles and she wanted to join them. I believe traditions only matter if you want them to, but if you're relaxed your wedding will be better.

When I asked the women in my focus groups, the majority – no matter where they fell on the 'feminism spectrum' – wanted their dad to be approached before a proposal. When I probed further, it turned out that for most it wasn't because they believed they were being passed from one household to another; it was a mark of respect. One of the Sugababes said, 'I don't have a relationship with my dad, but I would be upset if my future husband didn't ask my mum before he proposed. To me, that would be his way of saying, "You who raised this woman deserve to be honoured and included in this decision."'

Others wanted some elements of their tradition but not all. One woman said she'd like her father to walk with her down the aisle but not to present her hand to her husband-to-be, as that felt too much like a transaction between two men. Another said that in Nigerian culture a man comes knocking for the woman and pays a dowry to her family, but she would prefer it if he just asked permission from her parents, because: 'There's no price you can put on me, so let's not bother, babes.' (And that's your recommended dose of 'absolute queen' for the day.)

I believe marriage is an important part of the Christian faith. I also believe that, as long as you have a ceremony that honours God, the cake cutting, bouquet tossing, wearing white, being given away, doing speeches and choice of first dance are all a matter of preference. I'd be surprised if we got to heaven and found out God had strong feelings on the matter. But when it comes to the actual marriage, that's when things really do get interesting.

Marriage

Insignificant, unmarried women

First, it would be remiss of me if I didn't point out that the Church responds in a very different way to men who are single than it does to women who are single, particularly once they're out of their twenties and thirties. This will be a small section, because I've already written a whole book on the topic.[1] But it came up time and time again in the focus groups. It's felt inside and outside of the Church. In her short manifesto, *We Should All Be Feminists*, Chimamanda Ngozi Adichie says: 'A woman at a certain age who is unmarried, our society teaches her to see it as a deep personal failure. And a man, after a certain age isn't married, we just think he hasn't come around to making his pick.'[2]

Church should be a haven away from these worldly expectations. Being single is affirmed in the Bible; not just for men, but for women too. For some reason we've got the message twisted. Author Beth Allison Barr was told by leaders of a high school event that God designed women specifically to be wives who devote themselves to their husbands.[3] And back in the days of the Reformation, Martin Luther said: 'The work and word of God tell us clearly that women must be used for marriage or prostitution.'[4] Erm… what did Martin Luther just call me?

In my Sugababes focus group, one woman, who is single in her forties, explained: 'People in church assume that I'm single because I'm problematic or I'm too career-driven. They put these assumptions on me without even knowing my character, and they're absolutely nothing to do with me.' In reality, there are many reasons why a woman – or man – in the Church might be single, some of them based on the individual, some on society and some on the Church. If you're passionate about this as an issue, you're in good company. Check out my first book, *Notes on Love*, for more.

Complementarianism versus egalitarianism

Right, on to marriage. As I said, I am not married, but I do believe it's important to understand the Church's different approaches to marriage – and that your future partner may have a strong preference – before you get into a relationship. You may feel there are some ideologies that just aren't compatible with yours, and it's better to know before you've said 'I do' than to realise on your three-month anniversary.

Very broadly, we've got two camps: complementarianism and egalitarianism. Much like the word 'feminist' or 'Christian', the ins and outs of these terms vary greatly from person to person and household to household. On the whole, if someone says they are egalitarian, you can be pretty confident that what they mean is they believe the Bible mandates gender equality and equal responsibilities in the family unit and also in church leadership. Christians for Biblical Equality define egalitarianism as: 'All believers – without regard to gender, ethnicity or class – must exercise their God-given gifts with equal authority and equal responsibility in church, home and world.'[5] There are a fair number of people – often the ones we would broadly say were 'conservative' – who don't believe this is biblical. It will come as no surprise to you that I'm not in that camp.

By contrast, after speaking to a wide range of people, I've concluded that the term 'complementarian' varies far more widely, and you can't know exactly what someone means by it until you've asked a few more questions. According to the Council on Biblical Manhood and Womanhood, complementarianism:

Affirms that men and women are equal in the image of God, but maintain complementary differences in role and function. In the home, men lovingly are to lead their wives and family as women intelligently are to submit to the leadership of their husbands. In the church, while men and women share equally in the blessings of salvation, some governing and teaching roles are restricted to men.[6]

Adrian Warnock, writing for the website Patheos, sees the whole system as a spectrum and puts forward this model:[7]

	Roles in Church	Roles in Home	Roles at Work
Patriarchal	Different	Different	Different
Strong Complementarian	Different	Different	Similar
Moderate Complementarian	Some differences	Different	Some differences
Soft Complementarian	Similar	Similar	Identical
Moderate Egalitarian	Same in theory	Similar	Identical
Strong Egalitarian	Identical	Identical	Identical
Extreme Feminism	Different	Different	Different

Here's your cheat sheet for working out which of these you subscribe to:

Patriarchal

Those with a patriarchal view feel that men should be in a position of authority over women. Some aren't keen on a woman working and, at the most extreme end, even question if women need university-level education. Their justification for this is that there are fundamental differences between the sexes. This view has, in some cases, been used as an excuse for abusive behaviour.

Strong complementarianism

The pillars of strong complementarianism are that men and women are equal in status before God, but they naturally have different skill sets, so should take on roles that are different but 'complement' each other. Women in the workplace are often considered reasonably equal, although they are encouraged to lead in a way that doesn't 'dishonour' a man's masculinity. But with this model, women's leadership in the Church is out of the question and their priority should be homemaking and motherhood.

Moderate complementarianism

When we move on to the moderate complementarian view, we're looking at men who believe their role is to lead the household, but through becoming a servant rather than a boss. While men believe they have biblical authority over women, it's not to be used to dominate or oppress in any way. It requires men to regularly make sacrifices for their families. It's somewhere around this point that a man would acknowledge that there are limits to a woman's submission, for example in the bedroom. They may also agree that women need to be wise in how they follow, rather than exercising blind servitude. There are some leadership roles granted to women here. Although it's unlikely they would be allowed to be the primary leader of a church, they may be invited to speak from the front on some topics.

Soft complementarianism

In the soft complementarian category, people often consider that there is no difference between men and women in the workplace. The primary leader in church is still a man, but there could be women who serve as elders and help with the running of the church. A woman's husband (if she has one) will always take the lead, although at home there could be chat of 'mutual submission' (which Paul writes about in Ephesians 5), with the vague idea that a man leads his wife without a set formula for how that plays out in practice.

Moderate egalitarianism

Moderate egalitarians recognise that there are times in the Bible when God gives different instructions to men and women, but will view these through a lens of total equality. Roles at home are equally divided and the decision on who (if anyone) stays at home to raise children is taken based on circumstances and not sex. The marriage is democratic, and in church men and women are theoretically equal, although the key positions in a church may still end up being taken by men.

Strong egalitarianism

Strong egalitarians have no leader in their marriage; it's either run in complete equality, or each takes turns in leading and being led. At work and in church, gender is irrelevant and people will be appointed to positions based on their qualifications. Plenty of people in this camp would be cool with describing themselves as a 'feminist'.

Extreme feminism

Let's move on to extreme feminism where, in response to years of systemic oppression, women devalue men. They believe that, in compensation for what's passed, women should be elevated over men in the home, workplace and potentially Church too – although I've never actually heard of a Christian subscribing to this idea.

Complementarians often believe that egalitarians are rejecting the truth of the Bible, while egalitarians often believe complementarians oppress women and put them at risk of abusive behaviour. But I truly believe we can find a way to disagree well, provided there is absolutely no abusive behaviour exhibited in our relationships.

That said, I'm heartbroken by the pain and suffering I have seen inflicted on women, particularly married women, under the guise of biblical manhood. Ed Stetzer, Executive Director of the Wheaton College Billy Graham Center, affirms what many women have known for years: the Venn diagram of complementarian and misogynist has a significant overlap, which men and women of character from within the complementarianist movement must address.[8] *New York Times* bestselling author of *A New Gospel for Women* and *Jesus and John Wayne*, Kristin Kobes Du Mez, says of complementarianism: 'It was a vision that promised protection for women but left women without defense, one that worshiped power and turned a blind eye to justice, and one that transformed the Jesus of the Gospels into an image of their own making.'[9]

I see marriages that operate under all levels of this spectrum (excluding the extremes), and I can see that the majority are loving, caring and respectful. But we're humans and we have scope to really get things wrong. When it comes to power in relationships, we must exercise the highest levels of caution and accountability. Ultimately, no matter what you believe, the humility and servant heart of Jesus should be your first example when it comes to the treatment of others. I believe that can be exercised well within both a complementarian and an egalitarian relationship.

The dynamic between husband and wife

Martin Luther said: 'If women get tired and die of bearing, there is no harm in that; let them die, so long as they bear; they are made for that.'[10] Is anyone else starting to really dislike this guy?

The vast majority of people no longer believe that a wife is her husband's property. We're past that, right? I don't know if everything about the way we behave always reflects that progression though. I was on holiday in Croatia a couple of years ago. I was walking down the street after dinner with a friend of mine called Tim. He's tall and handsome, and bears an uncanny resemblance to Disney's depiction of Prince Charming. It was a busy evening, with lively bars and restaurants and a strong cohort of Brits abroad, doing their Brits-abroad thing – I can say that because I used to (in the years BC) be one of them. A group of six lads, all around twenty-one, had clearly enjoyed many of the delights of Split and were on their way to continue their evening's indulgence when they walked up behind us. One of these guys, completely harmlessly and definitely by accident, tripped me up. I didn't fall on my face – thank goodness – I just stumbled a bit and kept walking. Realising his mistake, the lad jogged a few paces forward and said to Tim, 'Er, sorry mate. I just kicked your missus by accident.' Tim looked at me, laughed and told the bloke it was fine. He then swiftly directed me around a corner in anticipation of my response.

I was in a good mood – I was on holiday, after all – so it became a source of great hilarity for the rest of the trip. The assumption that we were a couple was totally natural given that it was just the two of us walking together. But the assumption that any slight on me should be justified to my partner rather than me directly… I mean, come on. In fairness to our 18–30s booze-cruise mate, Tim is pretty broad, so if there was one of us to pacify in the interests of safety, I can see why he chose Tim. Either way, that's something we can add to the 'stop it now, please' list.

I'm of the egalitarian persuasion, but in my focus groups I found the women to be roughly 50/50. Those who believed in male headship were specific about the limits of that dynamic.

The women who said they would be comfortable with their husband being the head of their household and family said that they would only ever marry a man who clearly valued, appreciated and prioritised their opinion. One of these women, who is the CEO of a charity, said: 'A good leader always consults their team. When I'm leading in business, I will let everybody have their opinion and I will let everyone run with their strengths. I'm secure enough in my skills and leadership that I don't need to dominate people. I expect the same from a husband.'

When we talked about the biblical foundation of that belief, the main verses we spoke about were Ephesians 5:21–33:

Submit to one another out of reverence for Christ. Wives, submit yourselves to your own husbands as you do to the Lord. For the husband is the head of the wife as Christ is the head of the church, his body, of which he is the Saviour. Now as the church submits to Christ, so also wives should submit to their husbands in everything. Husbands, love your wives, just as Christ loved the church and gave himself up for her to make her holy, cleansing her by the washing with water through the word, and to present her to himself as a radiant church, without stain or wrinkle or any other blemish, but holy and blameless. In this same way, husbands ought to love their wives as their own bodies. He who loves his wife loves himself. After all, no one ever hated their own body, but they feed and care for their body, just as Christ does the church – for we are members of his body. 'For this reason a man will leave his father and mother and be united to his wife, and the two will become one flesh.' This is a profound mystery – but I am talking about Christ and the church. However, each one of you also must love his wife as he loves himself, and the wife must respect her husband.

For the women I spoke to, the protection came from verse 25 onwards. If the man is supposed to 'give himself up' for his wife, as Christ did for the Church, then we're talking sacrifice to the level of death. The burden Jesus carried on behalf of the Church, and the punishment he took on in its place, is the most selfless act in human history. In every way, he gave and served far beyond reason, and it remains astonishing.

They also put caveats on their complementarianism by saying that they would always expect their husband to respond to them out of reverence for Christ. One woman said: 'To be clear, I am submitting to my husband on the condition that he is submitting to Christ. If he's not following Jesus, I'm not following him.'

Another added: 'If your husband really is living out that model of Christ's headship in the Church, submission will be easy. There's also an element of security in that because, when it's done properly, there's no space for any abuse of that headship.'

Do you know what? Even though it's not where I've landed, I like the theory. I'm tired. I've spent years making decisions for myself, driving things forward, praying and listening for direction in my life. To imagine that someone I loved and trusted, who was willing to lay down their life for me in servitude to Christ, would take over that responsibility feels like a long hot bubble bath for my anxiety. Although arguably, that attitude could be an abuse of the lack of responsibility. Hard to say without testing it out. And to be fair, just having someone to share decisions with would make a huge difference.

What scares me about the idea of marrying someone under this premise, or when one of my friends does, is that no man (or woman) is perfect. He will get things wrong – sometimes in a minor, correctable way, but sometimes not. We live in a world where six women are killed by a male partner or family member *every hour.* In the UK, one woman is killed by a man every two-and-a-half days.[11] The stakes feel too high to risk marrying someone with an unhealthy relationship with power and women.

The focus group I spoke to knew that. One said: 'I would only marry someone who was so immersed in Scripture that he fully understood the responsibility he had.' But, and I say this tentatively, how well do we know the people we marry? Is six months, a year, five years long enough to guarantee that their character will never significantly change? That they are so grounded in their faith they'll never be susceptible to corrupting influences?

Marriage is a risk, and sadly it's a bigger risk for women. I would be concerned that any negotiated level of complementarianism I agreed with a partner could be twisted somewhere down the line into something that is wholly not of God. I've seen it in Christian families in my life, and you may well have too. We need to be sure that we minimise the risk by not jumping the gun in dating and by really allowing ourselves time to get to know someone, and then more time to see them in a variety of different circumstances and under different pressures. Pacing a relationship pre-marriage could help some women to stay safe.

Women in the word

Genesis

It's all very well reading through the neatly laid out spectrum of beliefs in the previous Note and asking ourselves what feels right, but what's the point if we're not testing it against Scripture? A lot of people like the idea of egalitarianism, but feel it's not consistent with the Bible. I'm not a theologian. If this is something you want to dive into, speak to church leaders, read commentaries of the biblical passages, and engage with the ideas and opinions of people in all areas of the spectrum. There's always more to read and learn, which is what I've tried to do.

Let's start at the very beginning with Eve, created as a helper to Adam. Here's the verse: 'The LORD God said, "It is not good for the man to be alone. I will make a helper suitable for him"' (Genesis 2:18). So, what does 'helper' mean in this context? Are we talking, like, a golf caddy vibe? Or Assistant Head of Eden? Or assistant to the Head of Eden (shout out to my fellow *Office* fans)? In the original Hebrew, the word for helper here is *ēzer*, a word that is also used to describe God's relationship with Israel in Psalms 33:20 and 121:2. This is a pretty strong argument for it not indicating a person of lower standing. God is hardly Israel's assistant or caddy, is he?

Let's shuffle along a bit. Fast-forward to Adam and Eve's unfortunate encounter with a snake. They've eaten the costliest snack known to man, and that includes a service station meal deal. God goes for his stroll and can't find Adam and Eve because they've realised being naked isn't all it's cracked up to be. God is fuming. He doles out the punishments, including this for Eve: 'I will make your pains in childbearing very severe; with painful labour you will give birth to children. Your desire will be for your husband, and he will rule over you' (Genesis 3:16).

This is where we first see hierarchy between men and women: not in God's original design, but after the fall. This 'desire' for your husband and his 'ruling' over you was the result of sin. I don't believe it should be held up as God's ideal. In her book *Gender Roles and the People of God*, theologian Alice Mathews says:

> Hierarchy was not God's will for the first pair, but it was imposed when they chose to disregard his command and eat the forbidden fruit… Adam would now be subject to his source (the ground), even as Eve was now subject to her source (Adam). This was the moment of the birth of patriarchy. As a result of their sin, the man was now the master over the woman, and the ground was now master over the man, contrary to God's original intention in creation.[1]

The Paul brawl

Putting forward the argument for a complementarian marriage is a straightforward thing to do. You just have to list every passage in the Bible that calls for wifely submission. There are a few key verses to look up: Ephesians 5:21–33 (included in the previous Note), Colossians 3:18 ('Wives, submit yourselves to your husbands, as is fitting in the Lord') and 1 Peter 3:1–6:

> Wives, in the same way submit yourselves to your own husbands so that, if any of them do not believe the word, they may be won over without words by the behaviour of their wives… holy women of the past… submitted themselves to their own husbands, like Sarah, who obeyed Abraham and called him her lord. You are her daughters if you do what is right and do not give way to fear.

Some people take these at face value and conclude that wives should be in submission to their husbands. Some study them and wrestle with them and read commentaries, and conclude that wives should be in submission to their husbands. I took a look at this, and I didn't feel that way. We're all subject to confirmation bias – that is, when we want to believe something, we're primed to find proof of it. (It was the day my mate told me he had found a group of Christians online who were united in their collective 'God-given enjoyment' of BDSM that I realised if you look hard enough, you'll find someone to tell you what you want to hear.)

Complementarians may find the points below unreasonable; that may be because they're primed with their own confirmation bias or because I'm exercising mine. Either way, I'm open-handedly presenting you with the information I found compelling so that you can factor it into your own reasoning process.

Let's look at Ephesians 5 first: 'Submit to one another out of reverence for Christ. Wives, submit yourselves to your own husbands as you do to the Lord.' First (and this might be obvious to you, so sorry if it sounds patronising), the original letters from Paul weren't written with those handy subtitles to break up the sections by topic. They make it easier for us to read, as we're not staring at pages and pages of block text, but they are man-made, not divine addition. I've stuck with the NIVUK for my Bible references in this book – although I am partial to a bit of *The Message* when I'm in my 'girls gone wild' mood.

In the NIV, Ephesians 5 has a paragraph break before verse 21, with the heading 'Instructions for Christian households'. So the passage goes from mutual submission to the submission of wives. However, in the ESV – globally the second-most popular translation after the NIV – the paragraph break comes between verses 21 and 22, separating the mutual submission and wifely submission verses. This means that submitting to each other is presented as the rounding-off sentence in the previous section

'Walk in Love', and the verse on submitting to your husband is presented as a new topic under the heading 'Husbands and Wives'.

Does this placement matter? Well, yeah, kinda. Beth Allison Barr says:

> When this verse is read at the beginning of the Ephesians household codes, it changes everything. Yes, wives are to submit, but so are husbands. Instead of underscoring the inferiority of women, Ephesians 5 underscores the equality of women – they are called to submit in verse 22, just like their husbands are called to submit in verse 21.[2]

Could this be Paul's subversion of the Roman patriarchy rather than him reinforcing it? By starting the passage with mutual submission, the letter no longer signals that submission primarily belongs to the wife.

Here's how I think of it. Imagine I was writing a business management guide, and in it I said: 'Bosses, financially reimburse your employees.' You'd be, like, 'Yes, of course. Everyone knows that's how business works! Why did SPCK give Lauren this book deal?' But if I said: 'Business works best when you all financially reimburse each other,' you'd be, like, 'What's she on about? I'm not going to pay my boss money.' I'll admit the metaphor has its limitations. But it illustrates the obviousness of Paul's statement in verse 22 and the countercultural nature of his statement when read in the context of verse 21.

Beth Allison Barr says:

> Paul wasn't telling the early Christians to look like everyone else; he was telling them that, as Christians, they had to be different... When read rightly the household codes [of Ephesians 5] not only set women free... but they set all the

members of the household free from the 'oppressive elements' of the Roman world.[3]

Theologian Lucy Peppiatt explains that this is key to the Christian subversion of harmful Roman power structures. These codes were directed to all members of the household; they didn't just speak to the head of the household (who would always have been a man). She says they 'contain within them the overturning of accepted positions accorded to men, women, slaves, and children, and the expectations placed upon them'.[4]

And it's not just 'liberal Christian women' who agree with this. In his August 1988 apostolic letter, Pope John Paul II said:

> The author of the Letter to the Ephesians sees no contradiction between an exhortation formulated in this way and the words: 'Wives, be subject to your husbands, as to the Lord. For the husband is the head of the wife' (5:22–23). The author knows that this way of speaking, so profoundly rooted in the customs and religious tradition of the time, is to be understood and carried out in a new way: as a *mutual subjection out of reverence for Christ*.[5]

He goes on to suggest that using Paul's writings to justify female subordination would be equivalent to using those passages to justify slavery.

Even if I do see the merits of a soft, or even moderate, complementarian model, we've now reached what I consider the most compelling argument against accepting those verses at face value. I don't see how you can choose to acknowledge wifely submission but reject slavery when the two are listed together. When Paul speaks of wifely submission in Colossians 3:18, four verses later he issues instructions for slaves. And just before Peter addresses wives in 1 Peter 3, he addresses slaves in chapter 2.

Aside from a small cluster of racist extremists, no one is in support of the slave trade. These verses are read in the context of the time in which they were written and aren't used as a justification for slavery by right-minded people. We are encouraged to study, wrestle with and pray over the Bible; not just to take it as it appears at first glance. It is the living word. Some people will study it, wrestle with it, apply that context and still land on the side of complementarianism. We are all accountable for our own relationship with Christ, our own study of his word and our own actions. I believe there is a loving way to live with complementarian and egalitarian values, although I believe it becomes increasingly difficult and eventually impossible as you get to the extreme ends of the spectrum.

Ending a marriage

I've skipped a huge chunk of life here. I will highlight some of the issues for women when parenting, and the research around that, in my next Note. But if you want support in having a healthy marriage, the Marriage Course from Alpha is excellent.[6] Timothy and Kathy Keller have written several highly acclaimed books on the topic from a complementarian perspective – see *The Meaning of Marriage*.[7] See also *Grace-Filled Marriage* by my friend Claire Musters and her husband Steve.[8] For a funny read for Christian couples, try Kevin and Melissa Fredericks's *Marriage Be Hard*.[9]

I do want to say a final quick word on divorce, with a standard but important disclaimer: this is too big a topic for you to make a decision on your own, or after reading a paragraph and a half of this book. If you're considering divorce, you should definitely speak to several qualified people – therapists, marriage counsellors and church leaders. But I also know that time and time again, women have gone to their church to report abuse within their marriage and been told to stay put. It happened to a friend of mine, and she doesn't believe in God any more.

People often behave poorly with those they're closest to; we can all be difficult with the people we love. But there's a difference between not always responding with the patience you would like and abusive behaviour. No one enters a marriage with the hope or expectation of it ending in divorce, but for those who are being subjected to physical, mental, emotional, sexual or spiritual abuse in marriage, don't let anyone say that you can't leave. Walking away does not mean you're breaking your marital vows; the perpetrator is the one who's done that.

Happy families

No one would be surprised to hear that in the average family of a heterosexual couple, the woman tends to take on more of the domestic work than the man. How you as a couple decide to run your home and parent your children will be in no small way affected by where you sit on the spectrum in our last two Notes. I am not here to insult or contradict a setup that is uplifting and works for you.

The notion that a woman who stays at home to look after the family and the house has the less strenuous task is one I would completely dispute. There is no such thing as women who don't work – just women who don't get paid for work. Mum-of-two Jenny Tamas calculated the number of hours she spent breastfeeding her daughter in the first year and it came to approximately 1,500 litres of milk over 1,825 hours.[1] To put that into perspective, someone who works nine to five with twenty days' annual leave plus bank holidays will spend 1,856 hours in the office a year. That's just thirty-one hours more than Jenny spent with an infant clamped to her breast.[2]

The University of Michigan found that getting married creates an additional seven hours of housework for a woman.[3] The time spent doing domestic chores is most equal in men and women who are single. A Finnish study found that a single woman is likely to recover better from bypass surgery than a woman who is married, as the married woman is more likely to go straight back into working around the house, while a single woman is likely to rest for longer.

How can husbands help?

No husband wants to see his wife struggling to recover from bypass surgery because she's too stressed trying to sort the washing. But

I do worry that, in many Christian households, the burden is being left with the wife. I've seen far more examples of an equal partnership in the homes of my non-Christian friends.

I find it really difficult when I see a husband barely contributing when his wife is at her wits' end. If you subscribe to a complementarian model, where men and women have different roles in the house, then I would ask husbands to think. You're called to do all you can to lift her up and support her, to the point of laying down your life if necessary. You're called to use your headship to sacrifice for her. So, if your wife is truly struggling, what could you sacrifice in your life to take on more of the burden of unpaid work?

There is an increasing move towards offering more paternity leave to men, and I would encourage men to take their full allowance. Research suggests that each month a father stays on parental leave increases a mother's earnings.[4] Insurance company Aviva is widely praised for the introduction of its recent parental leave programme, where both mothers and fathers are offered six months on full pay. In the first year, new fathers took an average of twenty-one weeks' leave compared with just two weeks the previous year. My brother-in-law, who works at the company, was the first father to take this six-month leave in the UK. He and my sister now have four children, and this leave was invaluable for the care of their three older children while my sister was recovering and caring for their newborn. Other research published by the US National Library of Medicine in 2020 suggests that fathers who take paternity leave have a much closer relationship with their children.[5]

My brother-in-law is a hugely active parent, but my sister gets frustrated when other people praise him for picking the kids up from school and taking them to the park, or sitting and reading with them at night. They tell her she's lucky he's so 'hands-on'. We need to stop congratulating dads for contributing and expect it as a baseline. I'll never forget when a friend of a friend posted a selfie of himself and his child on Instagram and captioned it

'Daddy's babysitting!'. It's not babysitting when it's your own baby. I unfollowed him.

It's hard when you hear of a man in a family unit being so inflexible with his time. The fact is, raising children is a full-time job for both parents, not just the one who 'doesn't work'. In his book *Men: An investigation into the emotional male*, psychotherapist Phillip Hodson says: 'Men only need to change a little to gain great improvements in their relationships but they falsely see this change as considerable and resist it.'[6]

If you're married to a woman, I believe it's so important to give equal weight to her career – if that's what she wants. I would encourage men to share the work at home in all scenarios. Even if she is 'staying at home', she's still working. Don't see domestic chores as 'helping her', but rather as part of your role as a member of a well-functioning family.

The daughters of fathers who take on half of the housework are more likely to pursue their career aspirations and have higher self-esteem.[7] Their sons are more likely to believe men and women are equal, and when they get into their teenage years, those boys are half as likely to be violent as teenage boys who've been taught rigid views about gender and 'being a man'.

Angry men

You know how they say humans are the deadliest animals on earth? I googled it and it's not true. It's actually mosquitos. They kill 725,000 people annually through the transmission of malaria.[1] And there we were thinking we were hard. To be fair, humans come second, with a whopping 400,000 murders every year.

According to statistics in England and Wales, 93% of murderers are male.[2] So is it humans who are the second-deadliest killers in the animal kingdom, or is it men? Why are men statistically so much more likely to be violent than women? Research suggests: 'Aggression can result when a man experiences stress deriving from self-perceived failure to live up to masculine expectations (discrepancy) or when he maintains normative masculine expectations (dysfunction).'[3] In short, if a man fails to live up to toxic masculinity he can get angry, and if he does live up to it he can get angry. Oh good.

Of course, the person a woman is most likely to be physically hurt by is her husband or boyfriend. In the UK, 61% of women who are murdered are victims of their partner or an ex.[4] In addition, more than a third of all women worldwide have experienced physical and/or sexual violence at some point in their lives.[5] And, heartbreakingly, 137 women across the world are killed by a member of their own family every day. When left unchallenged, intimate partner violence has been known to lead to large-scale attacks. It was only in the 2010s that a connection was made between mass killers and a past history of domestic abuse.[6]

After UK protests about violence towards women in 2021, there was a huge outcry in the press and on social media for men to understand the threat women feel when they walk home at night.

But in response, #NotAllMen started trending online. Men wanted to remind women that they were dealing with a minority. Just to be clear, we know that not all men are violent, but when we're walking home in the dark, we can't tell the difference.

Not all men beat up their wives, grope women in nightclubs, ask for nudes or attack women on the street. But, as Marilyn French says in her 1993 book *The War Against Women*: 'As long as some men use physical force to subjugate females, all men need not. The knowledge that some men do suffices to threaten all women.'[7] Sadly, the threat is sufficiently real that #AllWomen have to protect themselves. I'm not being dramatic. We all know multiple women who've been groped in a club, we all know someone who's been in a physically abusive marriage and we all know someone who's been raped. So men, don't be annoyed when we get scared.

True beauty

KATIE PIPER OBE

Kate Piper OBE is a bestselling author, activist and broadcaster. In December 2009, following her personal experience, she founded the Katie Piper Foundation, offering a brighter future for all survivors of burns and scars.

I've had a complicated relationship with beauty – just like most women. Keeping up with what the world says is 'beautiful' is virtually impossible when the definition shifts depending on which country and culture you're a part of and the trends of the time. I was one of the noughties girls who over-plucked her eyebrows, only to have to draw on nice thick ones when the style changed.

At school we only had one another to compare ourselves to, and no one knew what they were doing. Everyone thought my blue eyeshadow and hair mascara looked great – it was the blind leading the blind. These days, teenage girls and grown women measure beauty based on what they see in the media, the celebrities who are put on the front covers of magazines, and the people they follow on Instagram and TikTok. The opportunity for direct comparison is too tempting and too difficult for most of us to resist.

To say that 'comparison is the thief of joy' is very cheesy, but sometimes clichés are there for a reason. I believe that every time we look at another woman and ask, 'Is she prettier than me?' or 'Is she thinner than me?' or 'Does she look younger than me?' we're damaging our relationship with ourselves and each other. It's a road that leads straight to misery.

When I was younger, I was told all the time that I was beautiful. I was a model and enjoyed attention from guys on nights out. Lots of people know that my life changed dramatically, along with my looks, when I was in my early twenties. Suddenly I saw how differently people are treated based solely on their outside appearance. It's hard to fully understand how different a person's life experiences can be when their looks change until you've lived both ways.

I was left with severe scarring on my face, and I could see from the way people looked at me that they were scared of something they didn't understand. Sometimes I just wasn't treated as a human. It became painfully clear that, to some sectors of society, your worth and value are tied up in how you look.

Back in 2009, I established the Katie Piper Foundation. It's the only charity in the UK dedicated to delivering rehabilitation for burns survivors and those living with severe trauma scarring. I wanted to give a lifeline to burns and scar survivors. At the launch event I gave a speech and said: 'One of the hardest things about being disfigured is getting over how other people view or react to you. If together we can change that, we will take away half the battle.'

When it comes to beauty, I believe we all need to be challenged to look beyond the pages of magazines and see that it comes from richness and variety. And that goes for how we look at the beauty within ourselves too. We can be our own worst critics when it comes to our looks, and we should be our own biggest champions.

How others see us is often based on their own insecurities and fears. Remember, we're all subjected to the same 'perfect' images, so even with all this new technology and countless opportunities for connection, it's still the blind leading the blind!

The thing is, none of that is *real* beauty. God says that all of those surface-level 'beautiful' things will be lost (Proverbs 31:30). That's not the beauty he's looking for from us, and it's not the beauty we should be looking for in ourselves. I find drive, ambition and confidence so beautiful. Someone who communicates well and puts others at ease with a high level of emotional intelligence is beautiful. Someone who clearly has strong self-awareness and empathy, in my opinion, radiates pure beauty.

Let's focus on the grace, kindness, honesty and authenticity that are stunningly beautiful when we see them in another person, and let's celebrate and grow those things in ourselves.

When it comes to beauty, I believe we all need to know two things. First, what the world says is beautiful is not what is truly beautiful. Physical appearance will change and develop in time, away from what society says is the ideal. But that change, in itself, is beautiful.

Second, if beauty really is 'in the eye of the beholder', we the beholders get to choose whether we see it or not. Rather than looking for the perfect pout and the right-sized eyebrow – whatever that is – let's see it in every face and in every heart. Let's choose to reflect the beauty others put out back on to them. Let's celebrate the many ways we look different rather than encouraging everyone to look the same. And that means choosing to see the beauty in ourselves and our unique differences too.

A womb with a view: the way we look at women

It was my third year of going to Christian festivals. I had just about got used to 'camping for Christ'. It was the last evening of the conference, after three nights of broken sleep and four days of stuffy-shower-block ablutions. I was in the bar tent when I spotted a friend in the corner with a group of his mates. He was part of the team that had rigged up the site, and he was with the other roadies. I went over to say hi, and we ended up going off to have a proper catch-up. The next morning I woke up in my tent with the usual sweat patch on my sleeping bag and a text on my phone from the same friend. He said there was a bacon sandwich with my name on it if I headed to his Winnebago in the staff area. So, head to his Winnebago I did.

I was sitting in the driver's seat, tucking into a bacon bap with not nearly enough ketchup and chatting to him about how he watched *Love Island* on the tiny campervan telly, when there was a knock on the door. He answered, leaving the van door open, which obscured me from view as I was chowing down in the driver's seat. I heard a male voice say, 'Where did you get to last night? Did you have fun with shorty fatso?' My mate obviously performed some sort of gesture to indicate that I was within earshot, and the visitor said, more quietly but still audibly, 'Oh, really? Okay, I'll catch you later,' and walked off. That was the first and only time since I'd left an all-girls' secondary school that I heard someone call me fat. I don't think I should have to specify this – because even if I were morbidly obese, people shouldn't speak like that about each other – but I'm *not* fat. My actual size, weight and BMI are irrelevant. I'm not super-slim, I'm not super-big, and that's it. I am 5ft 3, however, so the statement wasn't completely factually inaccurate. But it was mean.

Why do people – men and women – feel the need to comment on a woman's weight or her looks at all?

Mirror, mirror on the wall

Women's looks are more spoken about, valued and judged than men's. But what readers of this book will no doubt be hoping is that this worldly evil doesn't find its way into the Church. I've got bad news for you...

Single women in particular feel acutely self-conscious in a church environment. When I was interviewing men for my last book on dating in the Church, I had one man confirm that, as there were so many more women than men in the community, he expected to date someone significantly better-looking than him. This attitude is disheartening for women at best and damaging at worst.

Many people feel that the 'perfect Christian woman' is slim, with a bouncy ponytail and bright eyes. You've already got a picture in your head, so I don't have to colour it in for you. But very few people look like that. Even the women who seem to look like that often don't when they're just hanging out at home.

Once again, this injustice is often felt more keenly by women of colour. One of the Black women from my focus groups told me that she felt more 'othered' in church for her appearance than in any secular environment. She said:

I come from a creative background and career, and I have always been able to freely express myself whether people like it or not. I've always had natural hair, and in church I feel I've been looked down on because of it. It doesn't matter whether I've been in a 'Black church', 'white church' or any other type.

I have always felt that I'm more oppressed in the Church than anywhere else because I don't look like the type of 'attractive Christian girl' church men want.

Natural hair doesn't just affect women in church, but in the workplace too. Mary Ann Sieghart says: 'The bad news for black women is that those with natural hair are rated as less competent and less professional than those with straightened hair.'[1]

Chine McDonald agrees, and in *God Is Not a White Man* she explains that in church circles the expectation of 'femininity' from the women often carries a subtle undercurrent of racism. She says: 'Women have a role to play as helpers, homemakers and hotties; in each of these roles, it is femininity that is prized. But in subtle ways this femininity only refers to a particular type of woman: a white woman.'[2]

This is not just the sentiment of a few Black women who've been spurned and can't find a husband. Chine's married, for a start. It's the feeling of an outrageous number of women, and is felt more strongly as skin colour gets darker. This is supported by evidence that darker-skinned women receive fewer matches on dating apps.[3]

In John Piper and Wayne Grudem's book *Recovering Biblical Manhood & Womanhood*, the authors say that women shouldn't be physically muscular. They suggest that women who look this way 'may beget arousal in a man, but it does not beget several hours of moonlight walking with significant, caring conversation'.[4] You thought the postman comment was bad and then you heard that. When I read it, I couldn't help but think of the racial implications of this statement. I'm sure the authors hadn't thought of it and didn't deliberately mean to be more oppressive to Black women over others, but research shows that women of Black ethnicity have, on average, leaner body mass than women of other ethnicities. They're naturally more muscular.[5] Who is anyone to say where women should sit on that spectrum? Later you'll hear from Abigail Irozuru, who is an incredible woman of God and is also muscular. This is very much a result of her lifestyle and job as an Olympic athlete. If a man approached her because she 'begot arousal in him' and didn't think her worthy of 'several hours of moonlight walking with significant, caring conversation', not only would he not get very far with her, but he would also have me and several hundred other women from her church and community to answer to. You've been warned.

Women may be treated as commodities in the world, but single women are treated as low-value commodities in the Church. And it's got to stop.

Modest is hottest

People love to tell women how to dress. When I was nineteen, I went into a Christian bookshop and asked for a book on sin. I hadn't been going to church for the last six years, but I knew I needed something. I knew I needed help. I was already drinking heavily, and although I wasn't addicted to drugs at that point, things were looking ropey. The woman in the shop handed me a picture book called *Who is Jesus?* and said that was more appropriate. I bought it out of awkwardness (very British of me), but also grabbed an actual book on sin called *The Enemy Within*.[6] She wasn't impressed, but sold it to me anyway. As I started walking away, she said, 'Christians don't dress like that, you know.' I was wearing a pair of jeans and a strappy top with a lace trim. I didn't go back into any Christian environment for the next five years.

Christian women are told that they are responsible for a man's lust; that if they are objectified and sexualised by a man, they should start by addressing what they are wearing. Kat Armas says: 'I wonder, What if Christian men and women retrained their minds to appreciate the strength and beauty in a woman's body without seeing it merely as a cause to stumble, or worse yet, as a one-dimensional object suitable simply for pleasure or procreation?'[7]

Jesus told men that if they looked at a woman lustfully, they should gouge out an eye and throw it away (Matthew 5:29), not update the Church's guidelines on skirts above the knee. Kat Armas goes on to say: 'Perhaps the problem lies in the system that hypersexualized them and deemed them inappropriate simply for existing and moving the ways that they do.'

On an associated but different note, I've heard plenty of people with opinions about what is and isn't appropriate for women to wear, but I've never heard someone stop another Christian in church and ask if anyone was exploited in the making of their clothes. What are we saying about our priorities?

The trophy wives

In 1999, just twelve weeks after giving birth to her first son Brooklyn, singer Victoria Adams (soon to be Beckham) went on magazine TV show *TFI Friday*, where host Chris Evans asked her if her weight was back to what it had been pre-pregnancy. She said it was, and he brought out a set of scales to check, live on telly.[8]

We know the world expects perfect trophy wives, and prizes their looks above all else, but not the Church, right? Surely the Church is better. I hate to, once again, be the bearer of bad news...

Many people I spoke to in my focus groups felt there was more overt objectification of wives in the Church than in any other environment, excluding maybe a Vegas casino or a convention of Fortune 500 men aged over seventy. On top of this, many Christian women felt that men were fed a prosperity-gospel message about the trophy wives they deserved for good behaviour.

Megachurch pastor Mark Driscoll once told his congregation:

It is not uncommon to meet pastors' wives who really let themselves go; they sometimes feel that because their husband is a pastor, he is therefore trapped into fidelity, which gives them cause for laziness. A wife who lets herself go and is not sexually available to her husband in the ways that the Song of Songs is so frank about is not responsible for her husband's sin but she may not be helping him either.[9]

He later apologised for this comment. But the sentiment is held by many men in the Church that a wife must meet her husband's criteria for beauty throughout her life; and that she must satisfy him in bed. In her book *The Excellent Wife: A biblical perspective*, Martha Peace says: 'The husband should be so satisfied that even if another woman entices him, he won't be tempted.'[10] But the same isn't asked of men. A man's body or sexual technique isn't blamed if a woman cheats. If a woman cheats on her husband, it's her fault. If a man cheats on his wife, surely that can't also be her fault?

Women are left between a rock and a hard place. Be sexy and satisfy your husband so he won't cheat. But don't be sexy and cause men to lust after you so that, if married, they will have cheated on their wives in their hearts. Maybe this is why choosing what to wear can be so complicated.

All of this doesn't bode well for the 'in sickness and in health' vow that many make when they get married. What if your wife becomes unwell and her body changes? What if she loses her hair? These things can happen. What happens more often is that a woman gets pregnant and her body changes dramatically. Why is a dad bod sexy but a mum bod isn't, when the mums are the ones who carry the child?

Something that happens to 100% of wives is that they age. Many women are terrified of ageing, of their skin starting to line and their metabolism slowing down. More than 90% of Botox users and 92% of cosmetic surgery patients are female.[11] Men are silver foxes who age like a fine wine, or so the story goes, and women are old hags who age like a pint of milk.

This idea of how women should look, and even how they should service their husbands, has been hugely exacerbated by the prevalence of pornography.

Porn

I hate porn. I'm really trying not to swear in this book, but if I were going to it would be here. I honestly hate it. It normalises unobtainable female bodies with perfect tans, pert breasts and no body hair. A huge amount of the material online is non-consensual, as trafficked women are forced to perform for others' gratification. Women are beaten, made to take part in activities they don't want to and held against their will in the production of this 'entertainment'. You can read countless reports from actors who were formerly part of the porn industry, relating horrific stories of abuse, threats and humiliation. See 'Fight the New Drug' for a few examples.[12]

I was told one story about a fourteen-year-old boy and girl who were having sex for the first time. The girl found it so painful that she was in tears. Once they had finished, the girl asked the boy why he didn't stop when he saw her crying, and he answered, 'Women always cry during sex.'

One of the most viewed interviews I've done for the show I present on dating app Salt's website was with Natasha from the Naked Truth Project.[13] Sadly, I think this is because it has the word 'porn' in the headline which, given that it's such a heavily searched term, means the video has excellent search engine optimisation. In the video, Natasha points out that there is no time limit on consent when it comes to porn. If a woman consents to being filmed and watched when she is eighteen, she may not consent to that same video being watched when she is twenty-five. As far as I am concerned, as soon as a person withdraws their consent for you to watch them having sex, you are taking part in sexual assault.

But this doesn't affect the Church, right? Oh dear, hold tight because this may be another blow…

A survey found that 70% of men and 30% of women in the churches polled watched porn at least once a month.[14] Another study found that more than 20% of churchgoing men believed they were addicted.[15] One in five youth pastors and one in seven senior pastors were found to use pornography regularly. It is infecting our churches, our relationships, our social dynamics and our marriages. And it has got to stop.

I could go on about this for pages, but the final point I'll make is that porn is racist. There are countless examples where porn has eroticised and exoticised women of colour. During the Black Lives Matter protests in 2020, one of the most popular pornography websites in the world, Pornhub, posted a statement on social media standing against racism. But you could still peruse many examples of racial stereotyping in its Ebony category, such as 'White Guy Tames Angry Black Woman' and countless videos depicting Black women in bondage or slavery.

You have to believe me – by watching porn you are not only damaging yourself, your relationships and your own sex life, you are fuelling an industry that takes what it can from people without any regard for their humanity. It is, and I mean this literally, soul-destroying evil.

Does Christ offer freedom from this?

I'll keep this short and sweet. Yes. The Bible presents us with a realistic and affirming view of female beauty. Proverbs 31 warns against prioritising looks in your partner: 'Beauty is fleeting, but a woman who fears the Lord is to be praised' (31:30).

It does not say that women are expected to maintain their youthful appearance for the whole of their lives – just as it doesn't expect men to. But it instructs women and men to continue to find the beauty in one another. Proverbs 5 tells men to rejoice in the wives of their youth, and to always be intoxicated and satisfied by them. It doesn't tell women to always *look like* the wives of men's youth.

How to make sure godly men *can't resist* you

Seven steps to being the perfect church girl
#ChurchCuties #toptips

Hi guys, Sophia here!

Welcome back to my YouTube channel, Soph's Spiritual Sistas! I've had a lot of messages from my followers asking for this video, so I thought it was time to give you guys what you want. Today, I'm going to be sharing my complete seven-step guide to being the perfect church girl. I know that a lot of my followers are trying really hard to get this right, but end up going off track. So my seven tips should help. All right, keep cups and cardigans at the ready, let's get into it...

Step one – pay attention to your skincare
The golden rule when it comes to your skin is to never look old. Keep wrinkles or any weathering at bay with creams. Not just cocoa butter – I'm talking a full-on regime of serums, ointments and deep moisturisers. It may cost a fair bit, but turning back the clock doesn't come cheap.

Step two – use make-up wisely
Getting your make-up right is really important. A Christian girl never wears a rouge lip, a smoky eye or any kind of eye-catching facial art. Oh no – it's time to ditch every Urban Decay palette you ever bought. The key to your make-up is to make sure you always have smooth skin and a lovely dewy glow so that anyone

who looks at you, particularly a man, will say, 'She just looks so beautiful without make-up.' The amount of time and make-up required to create this look isn't relevant, as long as your efforts are undetectable.

Step three – make sure you exercise
A perfect girl is a pert girl. The best way to get there is via Pilates. I like to go to class and pray between poses. You can also run, but take care not to be seen sweating or with your hair all frazzled and poking out at the sides. It's so unsightly. Again, you want a gentle glow at all times, and tuck that hair under a cap if you can't guarantee it'll stay sleek. Whichever route you take, let's make sure you get – and stay – thin. And I don't mean just thin around the waist. It's super-important to stay slimline all over – curves are really quite vulgar.

Step four – dress demurely
Obviously, the key element in a Christian woman's appearance is what she chooses to wear. We're looking for the perfect balance of complete modesty and unintentional sexiness. I've found the best way to do this is to cover up in jeans and a high-necked jumper, but make sure both are tight enough that no one could accuse you of being fat. A pair of over-the-knee boots on top of the jeans often gives just the right hint of hotness.

Step five – be pure
Men, particularly in the Church, love it when they're more experienced than you, so don't put him off by telling him about your exes. Have you had a boyfriend before? No. Did you ever kiss anyone before me? No. Have you ever had any kind of physical intimacy – you know, doing bits and that? No. Nice and simple. Remember, his answers may not be the same, but don't hold that against him. Men are super-physical, and boys will be boys after all.

Step six – act naive

When you're speaking to a man, make sure you laugh at all his jokes, and when he talks to you on any topic, pretend you don't know about it, so he can tell you. You could ask him to explain something in politics or sport. Or if you want to keep it simple, just ask him what one of the words he said means. Then, once he's finished, comment on how smart he is. Maybe throw in an 'I don't know how you know all this'. Men love it when they can teach you new things.

Step seven – know the Bible, but not too well

The perfect Christian woman is godly and reads the Bible, but let's not go overboard. You don't want to be reciting Scripture and talking about passages in the original Greek. Instead, the perfect Christian girl keeps it simple. She knows all the sweet, cheerful verses of encouragement that fill her Instagram feed, surrounded by wildflowers. Plus, she knows Proverbs 31 – aka 'the manual'. If she ever needs a verse from anywhere else, she can ask one of the men in church; it's just another thing they'd be delighted to explain to her.

So that's it, guys – I hope you enjoyed my seven tips. Comment below and let me know which one was your favourite. I release new videos every Monday and Thursday, so hit 'like' and 'subscribe' for more from Soph's Spiritual Sistas! Byeeeee!

Sexual healing

The Church is not a natural place to go for sex advice. When I was young, people turned to *More* magazine or their mates' older brothers for information. Teaching on the mechanics of sex and anatomy is important, but that is probably best delivered in an awkward Year 8 Biology lesson. Where I think the Church comes in is when discussing all the other things that come with sex: the emotional and hormonal response; its place as a physical expression of deep commitment and intimacy; and the shame, guilt or sense of obligation some people feel in relation to it.

If you were to ask someone who has been in church all their life what it has taught them about sex, they're likely to say, 'That you shouldn't have it.' Most people only discuss the issue at a church youth camp, when teenagers are told to keep it in their pants at all costs. And then it's just radio silence till the marriage prep course.

A friend of mine who got married recently, having abstained from sex until the big day, told me she suddenly felt really let down. She realised she didn't know enough about her own body and her own pleasure. All she knew was that sex was bad, but she suddenly had the thumbs-up to crack on. Going from chastity-belt-wearing purity pledge to marital vixen is one leap too far for a lot of Christians, and they feel they're letting down themselves, their husbands and the picture of mind-blowing sex they previously had, all at the same time.

This altar call for sensible and loving teaching around sex is so important in light of the highly publicised, damaging information propounded by some preachers. Former megachurch leader Mark Driscoll stood up in front of his congregation of thousands and said: 'Ladies, your husbands appreciate oral sex. They do. So, serve them, love them well. It's biblical.'[1] He went on to say, 'Ladies, let me assure you of this: if you think you're being dirty, he's pretty happy,' and later, 'Jesus Christ commands you to do this.' I'm sure that's enough to illustrate my point, but just because this is so unbelievably outrageous, he also said: 'Satan did not invent stripping. It's something that God intends for his daughters to do and his sons to enjoy.' He then explained that 'highly visual' men would go to strip clubs if they weren't being served in this area at home. Not on a podcast or in an article – in his sermon.[2]

It's not just misguided men who teach these things in the hope of getting their rocks off more often. Author and ministry leader Debi Pearl says: 'Wife, it is your God-ordained ministry to your husband to be his totally enthusiastic sex partner, ready to enjoy him at all times… If you don't score high points here, you are providing an opening for your husband to be tempted by other women.'[3] She also claims the Bible says that even physical pain is no excuse for a woman to take a rain check on sex.

It goes without saying that the pressure of this is insane. This sense of obligation is not going to get any woman in the mood for seduction. Prior to 1992, forced sexual activity within a marriage wasn't illegal; it was deemed lawful that a husband could enforce his right to sex on his wife because she had given 'ongoing consent' when she agreed to marry him.[4] The idea that it is a husband's right to have sex with his wife whenever he chooses is totally wrong.

In 1 Corinthians 7:3–5, Paul says: 'The husband should fulfil his marital duty to his wife, and likewise the wife to her husband. The wife does not have authority over her own body but yields it to her husband. In the same way, the husband does not have authority over his own body but yields it to his wife.' The Bible promotes a posture of mutual submission, whereby both sides are completely equal and both ask the question: 'What can I give?', not: 'What can I take?' or 'What am I owed?' or 'What do I deserve?'

Meanwhile, outside of church...

Those inside the Church don't just face the confusion of having to be either a virgin or a vixen – or the expectation that they should be both. They also have to navigate continually changing views around sex in the world.

For years, women's bodies have been used to sell things. It's a classic marketing ploy and a complaint of feminists the world over. Women are told they will be more attractive and sexually appealing if they buy the latest hosiery or cosmetics. Men are told that with the right watch or cologne they can have the pulling power of James Bond. In reality, most women don't want to have sex with James Bond – no one wants to share their bed with someone so overly reliant on gadgets.

There has been a shift in the advertising industry in order to tame feminism to a capitalist society. In *Against White Feminism*, Muslim writer Rafia Zakaria points out:

> Sex was made into a commodity which could be consumed by both men and women. And if sex was understood as a commodity that women were choosing to consume, then the morally problematic objectification of women could be replaced by the apparently morally neutral objectification of sex.[5]

This isn't the only unhelpful 'remedy' to the sexual objectification of women. Author of *Who Stole Feminism?* Christina Hoff Sommers says: 'Sexual liberation may not be going in the direction of eliminating the Other as a sex object; it may instead be going in the direction of encouraging women to objectify the male as Other, too.'[6] This is not the solution; an equality where we're all treated badly is not the one we want.

Sexual liberation as a concept comes with its own challenges. A by-product of the movement is that women aren't just feeling free to embrace sex; they're feeling obliged to. Rafia Zakaria says: 'I had no problem at all with people having rich, varied and fulfilling sex lives or even talking about them. My problem was specifically with the expectation of talking about them as some sort of passport to feminist legitimacy.'

Ironically, this means that the idea of having a lot of sex has become its own type of oppression. Feminist entrepreneur and author of *The Sex Myth*, Rachel Hills, spoke to hundreds of women who felt they had to pretend to be more sexual to fit in with the 'cool, hip feminists'. She says: 'True female sexual autonomy... needs to entail the right to confidently *not* have sex when it is unwanted or unavailable on the terms she might prefer.'[7]

Sexual liberation has done harm to many women, as did the sexual suppression before it. I have a friend currently writing her PhD on the effect of consensual but unwanted sexual interactions, and that's a survey group a lot of women would sit in. I've sponsored and mentored women in and out of the Church, and time and time again I hear stories of women agreeing to sex when they don't want it. I'm not talking about sexual assault. All the legal checks and balances have taken place, consent has been given and the man would probably be mortified if he found out her true feelings. But for some reason a lot of women say yes to sex they don't want. Women are socially conditioned to please those around them, especially men. It's what we've been told to do. It's what women's magazines say is fun.

Writer and campaigner Louise Perry, author of *The Case Against the Sexual Revolution*, lists some of the other challenges women face as a result of the sexual revolution.[8] These include the obviously higher stakes in pregnancy and the impact of hormonal contraceptives. She also points out the increased danger to women engaging in casual sex, given that when a man and woman are alone together for a sexual encounter, the women will almost always be the less strong and therefore the more physically vulnerable.

I'm not a prude. I think sex is great. But it's been used and commercialised and politicised and twisted to the point where people – particularly women – are suffering. Sex isn't just a physical act that doesn't mean anything, and deep down I believe even the most sexually liberated among us can see that. As Louise Perry points out, if sex had no significance beyond the physical, then sexual assault and rape wouldn't feel any different from other violent crimes. It's deeply intimate and personal. If sex isn't special, then sexual harassment and rape can't be given any kind of distinctive status as crimes either.

A better picture

We all know about the sexual revolution of the 1960s. It was all Woodstock and peace and love and fantasising about shagging one of the Beatles. But there was also a sexual revolution in the first century AD in the Roman Empire that doesn't get nearly as much airtime.

Around this time, Roman norms dictated sexual behaviour. This meant that virginity was prized in high-status women, who were married off young – once they hit sexual maturity. But there were also vast numbers of female slaves who were ruthlessly used for prostitution in order to allow rich men to 'let off steam'. Paying for sex was seen as a necessary outlet for men to prevent their lust from taking over and ruining society. In his book *From Shame to Sin: The Christian transformation of sexual morality in late antiquity*, Kyle Harper says of these enslaved women: 'The unfree body [bore] the pressures of insatiable market demand. In the brothel the prostitute's body became, little by little, "like a corpse".'[9] The men were also regularly involved in sexual relationships with underage boys, which went unchallenged and were accepted by society.

It's no surprise that the Romans expected chastity from women. Virtually all communities and cultures throughout time have done so in order to ensure that they know the paternity of their children. But where Christianity was radically different from the norms of the day was that chastity was expected of the men too. Louise Perry explains that early Christians didn't liberate women by allowing them to sleep around like men, but instead encouraged men to adhere to the same monogamy expected of women. According to Louise, research shows that most women are looking for monogamous relationships.

If the entire Roman world had embraced this idea, the brothels would have closed down overnight, and the practice of gaining a sexual outlet through the rape of slaves or children would have been over. The idea of this would have been wildly countercultural back in the day. But by demanding the same behaviour from men and women, Christianity offered liberation.

So how does this translate to our modern churches and relationships? First, we need to talk about sex more in church. It is not disgusting or shameful, so we need to find ways to encourage people to understand their bodies and not be ashamed of their desires. The fact is, whether you're having sex or not, you have a sex life. By keeping it in the dark, away from well-chosen accountability partners or close friends, you're more likely to get buried in shame.

Explaining the value of abstinence and waiting till marriage is important, but it's far from the only conversation the Church should be having. When people are preparing to get married – having heard 'don't touch' for their entire lives – we need to help them find a way to truly enjoy sex. Some couples may genuinely need some support in navigating the mechanics of the situation. I'll never forget the story in Adam Kay's *This Is Going to Hurt*, when doctors couldn't understand why a young married couple were struggling to conceive until it transpired that they had been rubbing his semen into her belly button. Or the man who told Dr Kay that he and his wife couldn't use condoms because there wasn't one big enough for his penis. After some investigation, it turned out he'd been trying to roll it over his testicles, too.[10]

Plenty of couples do a pre-marriage course of some kind offered through their church. But I think we also need to assign an older married couple to speak to them, both together and individually, about sex. To talk about expectations, about potential problems – which are common – about drinking cranberry juice on your honeymoon, about the difference between male and female pleasure, and the length of time it's likely to take before it gets really good.

Christy Bauman calls for churches to stop shying away from these conversations. She says: 'God's design for sex is obviously intentional and powerful, and I believe God has given us power through the holiness involved in the act of sex and pleasure.'[11] The Bible contains some wildly passionate depictions of sex. If you enjoyed the poetic seduction in Bridgerton, you should hear some of the imagery in Song of Songs. In *A Year of Biblical Womanhood*, Rachel Held Evans says: 'Where much of the Old Testament seems to regard female sexuality as something to be regulated and feared, Song of Songs unleashes a vivid and erotic expression of woman's desire.'[12]

There are plenty of Christian men who feel they've married a 'leaky tap' (see Proverbs 27:15) rather than 'sex on tap'. But it may be worth reminding everyone that good and frequent sex is not an entitlement; it is the fruit of a healthy, loving and nurturing relationship. If your partner was in an accident that rendered them paralysed and unable to have sex, that would be no reason to leave them. For better, for worse, in sickness and in health. Sometimes poor mental health can lead to a crippling loss of libido. Rather than pushing your partner into unenjoyable sex, taking a break without any pressure can be very helpful. It's nothing to feel ashamed or guilty about. Also, although an American doctor would sign a new mother off to have sex again six weeks after giving birth, research suggests it takes a woman's body two years to fully recover from labour. So be kind to yourself and allow yourself as long as you need to heal.

For the blokes who would like to be getting their rocks off more than they are – your wife will be far more attracted to you when you focus on the passionate and deep love you share for each other and your mutual desire, than when you're legalistically reciting verses that you believe entitle you to being serviced three times a week.

It's worth noting here that there are plenty of women who want to have sex more frequently than their husbands. This isn't shameful or dirty; everyone's libido is different. But just as I have suggested for men, there must be care and compromise rather than nagging when it comes to establishing a healthy middle ground in the bedroom.

The more secure, mutually uplifting and close your relationship is, the better the sex will be. The message from Paul in 1 Corinthians 7 (quoted above) is clear: sex is about husband and wife giving to each other; not about a husband taking from his wife. I really like the framework for this sketched out in the Torah and elaborated on in the rabbinic tradition. The Law of Onah outlines a husband's conjugal duties to his wife and specifies that he should think of her pleasure during the act and not just his own. It says that anyone having sex for selfish satisfaction without thinking of their partner's enjoyment is wrong. Sex should happen during times of joy, a man shouldn't force his wife to have sex, and a couple shouldn't have sex while they were arguing or drunk. It isn't to be used as a weapon for punishment, either through deprivation or through pushing it on the other. Sex is considered her right, not his – although she doesn't have absolute discretion to withhold it from her husband.[13]

A lot of this is just sensible, so why does it sound like some sort of sexual utopia to so many women? I honestly think the relief of knowing that they were protected by specifically laying out guidelines like this would help women feel so much freer to enjoy sex. Maybe it's time the Church offered at bit more support to couples.

Women and sporting bodies

ABIGAIL IROZURU

Abigail Irozuru is an English track and field athlete, specialising in long jump. She made her Olympic debut in the postponed Tokyo 2020 Games representing Team GB.

Body image

I was twenty years old when two security guards stopped me from entering a club. They told me I had to pay the cover charge because 'only females go in for free'. They may have been joking, they may have been serious, they may have been somewhere in between – I couldn't tell. But I vividly remember the conversation between them, debating whether or not I was 'a man in a dress'. Eventually they stepped aside, laughing, to let me enter the club after they had decided I was probably female.

Why did this happen? It turns out that a woman with 'man arms' didn't make sense to the nightlife security professionals of Tunisia. I was sporty and competitive as a child. Growing up, I kicked a football around with my cousins in the park, climbed trees, danced and joined all the clubs: gymnastics, trampolining, Girl Guides, netball, swimming, archery and more. I loved being active. And this desire to always be on the move shaped my physicality from a young age. I mean, I've had abs since I was eight years old!

I also grew up with my mum bemoaning my big feet (UK size 9.5) and muscular arms, adding to my self-consciousness that I was a deviation from the 'feminine ideal'. This consciousness, coupled with the Tunisian experience in 2010, led to a lot of self-loathing and a warped perception of 'feminine beauty' that, to this day, affects my perception of myself when I'm not on top form. But on good days, looking in the mirror at my muscular physique, I'm reminded of all the good that's come from my body.

I should introduce myself: I'm Abigail Irozuru, a British long-jumper of Nigerian heritage – both my parents were born in Nigeria. I've competed in track-and-field athletics since I was fourteen years old, first representing Great Britain in 2007. I finally achieved my Olympic dream when I competed for Team GB at the 2020 Tokyo Olympic Games, finishing eleventh in the final. Not bad, huh?

In my life, I guess there is always a tension between the feminine 'ideal' and who I am as a woman – feminine, strong and uniquely me. I've no doubt that this is a tension we are all familiar with in our own ways. The fact that we all worry we're not feminine or pretty or slim or curvy enough is why I want to highlight the importance of recognising the changing sociocultural standards imposed on us. Commentary on and policing of the female body – particularly by male-dominated institutions and governing bodies – is completely unnecessary and deeply damaging.

Eilish McColgan, the woman who set a Commonwealth Games record in 2022 for her 10,000 metres and took home the gold medal, serves as a clear example of the unfair treatment women in sport receive, particularly in comparison to their male counterparts. The athlete has been showered with criticism for being too thin, and therefore serving as a poor role model for young girls in sport. But I've never heard a single disparaging comment about the male athletes who are equally lean. She suffered this discrimination despite being very vocal about eating regular, balanced meals and maintaining her monthly periods – a good indication that you are not under-fuelling, which can be a particular challenge for endurance athletes.

The thing I find saddest of all is that these comments were mostly made by women! Dragging and shaming does not just indicate a lack of self-love; it shows a lack of understanding of the breadth and depth of God's love for us, collectively and individually. We're fully known and fully loved.

In the past couple of years we've seen 'well-intentioned' female officials loudly and humiliatingly encouraging Paralympic sprinter Olivia Breen to 'cover up', after deeming her running knickers 'too revealing' – despite these being her brand's uniform, and therefore out of her control. And the United World Wrestling federation banned young wrestler Latifah McBryde from competing in full-coverage modest uniform and hijab due to its 'safety risk and possible advantage'. It seems no one can decide whether we're too covered up or not covered up enough.

Hormones

Unfortunately, commentary and criticism around a female athlete's body – her size, shape or even what she wears – isn't the only challenge to contend with. There is increasing coverage of the discrimination, just as there is with equal pay and the harassment of women in sport, but an issue that is yet to have its day of reckoning is the relationship between female athletes and their hormones.

Some female athletes track their periods ten months in advance to see whether they'll be 'on' during their Olympic or Paralympic final. To be unlucky enough to hit the most challenging phase of her cycle during a key competition is a fate no female athlete or her team wants to deal with. It doesn't matter how much preparation you've done, periods around high-stress situations (for example, an Olympic final) are, more often than not, going to be worse than usual – early or late, more painful and heavier, with more debilitating symptoms. I have spoken with one female athlete who honestly believes her period cost her an Olympic medal, and I'm sure there are many more who feel the same way.

Like many women, plenty of athletes don't want to control their hormones because it messes with their body weight, moods and muscle/tendon health – and I'm one of them! Managing your period effectively is a science project you tinker with every month and hopefully hone ahead of key events. You have to figure out strategies around diet, nutrition, hydration, sleep and social interactions, mental and physical health, and training intensity for the various phases of your monthly cycle. This isn't a 'one and done' job; it is a perpetual process of monitoring, adapting and implementing. And even then it isn't fail-safe.

There are apps like Clue, FitrWoman and Samsung Health (thank you!) that help make the tracking and monitoring process a lot clearer, while providing valuable insights and updates on research in the area to help improve the way women manage their cycles and symptoms.

And what about pregnancy? Most female athletes feel that their sport puts that on hold. Until very recently, women were basically punished for getting pregnant – contracts were cut, funding was dropped, careers were scuppered. Few female athletes were in a position to make the choice of family versus career, as the choice was taken away from them by the corporations that financially supported them. And on occasion, when they did have that choice, some found themselves making the decision to terminate their pregnancy, feeling backed into a corner and forced to prioritise career over family.

In her book *Chasing Grace: What the quarter mile has taught me about God and life*, Christian runner Sanya Richards-Ross shares how she made this decision when she found out she was pregnant before the Olympics. She says: 'The truth is, it's not really an issue that's talked about – especially in sports. A lot of young women have experienced this. I literally don't know another female track and field athlete who hasn't had an abortion – and that's sad.'[1] My experiences aren't quite as extreme as Sanya's, as I do know athletes who haven't had abortions, but I know far too many who have. It is heartbreakingly common.

The choice of family versus career is a balancing act in most fields, but more often than not it is doable. Elite sport is still behind other industries in that regard. Yet, as frustrating as these experiences are, it's also inspiring to see women fighting for themselves, and for future girls and women in sport, to create positive, lasting change.

Badass women like Shelly-Ann Fraser Pryce, Allyson Felix and Serena Williams are just some of those leading the way. They fought convention. When Nike cut Allyson, she started her own brand. When Serena nearly died in childbirth, she brought more awareness to the prevalence of sky-high Black- and Brown-female mortality rates. And Shelly-Ann proves that pregnancy doesn't ruin your career; you can be a mum, break records and win medals.

Faith

My faith in God is paramount in my life, but it isn't the only faith that's important. You need faith in yourself as well – in the God-given gifts and talents you've been blessed with and have been faithful to nurture, and which you've used to uplift not just yourself but others too. Sport keeps teaching me that faith in yourself and your team is powerful too. Because if Shelly-Ann, Allyson and Serena hadn't believed in themselves and their unique voices, they might not have created such change.

Sport is my world, and I look at these women as examples of a beautiful intersection of faith and feminism. They inspire me to have faith in God and faith in myself – in the fullness of who I am. They use their womanhood and their platforms to express who God has created them to be. By being themselves they show the world, their daughters, us as fellow women, and particularly us as fellow female athletes: 'Look what we can do. And if we can do this, you can too.'

For me, feminism is standing out in the fullness of my womanhood – as an overtly muscular female athlete – and saying:

'This is me. I am still a woman. Even if this isn't how you see me through your limited view of the world, I am a woman. And my womanhood is a gift. It's because of my womanhood and femininity that I make waves in this world, defy convention and create tangible, lasting change to athletics contracts, medical efficacy, racial equality, gender pay gaps and terms around pregnancy.'

I wish twenty-year-old Abs had known her worth and beauty. She wouldn't have set foot in that club – the one she spent part of the night crying in. She wouldn't have refused to do press-ups for years to make sure her arms didn't get bigger, or avoided sleeveless tops and dresses because she was scared of the attention and comments.

Looking at these images of female empowerment in sport and knowing that God has given us all unique gifts and capacities for greatness helps me to realise that I can make an impact, I can make a change, simply by being me and standing up for my rights as a woman in my world. And so can you.

I hope you can be empowered to be your fullest self and shake off the constraints that have been placed on you by society, culture or a hurtful comment, because, like the women above, you'll change the world for the better when you do. See the value in yourself as a woman and use your unique God-given gifts. That's faith and feminism.

#ChurchToo

It *is* our problem

I sometimes approach churches to ask if I can speak to their congregations about the addiction recovery programme I run, and have often received this response from leaders: 'We don't have anyone with that problem here.' They flat out refuse to believe that in their congregation of a hundred or so people, one might be struggling to control a habit they don't know about.

I've said it before and I'll say it again: it is naive to believe that something happening in wider society isn't happening in your church. And, sadly, this includes sexual violence. A Christian friend told me she was at a party and went upstairs to the toilet. When she came out, a man – also Christian – pushed her up against the wall, kissed her and tried to grope her, despite her protestations. The next day he texted her to say he was sorry and explained his actions by saying that he had 'been hanging around with a lot of non-Christian girls recently'. Another shared how a man had picked her up for a date in his car, but instead of taking her to the bar, pulled over down a side road and tried to have sex with her. When she objected, he told her: 'You're saying no now, but I know that if I just did it, you'd like it.' The following day he was on stage playing drums at his church.

I speak in churches about addiction, not sexual assault, but sometimes it comes up, particularly if I open the floor to a Q&A. After one youth evening, a teenage girl came over to say it was the first time she'd heard a church speaker talk about sexual assault or consent. She wanted to know if someone would still want to marry her if she was assaulted, or whether she would be 'too impure'.

We think we don't need to educate men in church about consent, because men in church don't rape. We think of rapists as extreme, violent strangers who wait in dark corners for women to be walking alone, and anything that doesn't fit into that category is 'less harmful' or 'a matter of opinion'. In reality, most of us haven't grasped the actual criteria for informed consent.

You DO NOT have consent if:

- the person is below the legal age of consent;
- the person is unconscious;
- the person is intoxicated by any mind-altering substance, including alcohol;
- you have cajoled, coerced or coaxed someone into the situation;
- you have misrepresented your intentions to that person (for example, telling them you're interested in a long-term relationship when all you want is a one-night stand);
- you are in a position of authority over that person – meaning they might find it more difficult to say no (for example, a superior at work, a teacher or a church leader);
- the person has agreed to have sex using a specific type of contraception (for example, a condom), but you don't use it or you remove it part of the way through.

Additionally, you do not have the right to expect sex just because:

- the person came to your house;
- the person said they wanted to have sex with you earlier in the evening;
- the person had sex with you last week;
- the person is your husband/wife;
- you went to some effort to facilitate a sexual encounter (for example, booking a hotel room).

The second reason the Church needs to speak more about sexual assault is the injustice and inequality it reveals. Indigenous women in the United States are two-and-a-half times more likely to be sexually assaulted than other women.[1] According to the Institute for Women's Policy Research, 20% of Black women are raped in their lifetime – a higher share than among women overall.[2] Black women are two-and-a-half times more likely to be murdered by men than their white counterparts. And they experience significantly higher rates of psychological abuse – including humiliation, insults, name-calling and coercive control – than women overall.[3]

As if that wasn't bad enough, statistics show that Black women who report crimes of sexual assault or violence are less likely to be believed than their white counterparts. Women from the Latin American, Native American and African–American communities are less likely to seek out help from law officials and law enforcement.[4] For every Black woman who reports a rape, there are at least another fifteen who don't.[5] In addition, if a Black woman is assaulted by a Black man in her own community, she may feel she has betrayed the solidarity within her own racial group by reporting him. She carries the burden of wanting to uphold the collective unity in her group, rather than handing over a member of her community to a law enforcement system that has a long history of abuse, mistrust and neglect towards that group.[6] She also experiences the terror of leaving her own vulnerability to a majority-white justice system that has been known to show bias in handling crimes against minority groups.[7]

Sexual violence is often not about sex. It's about asserting and demonstrating power. This is horrific enough for a white woman, as the imbalance of control and power between men and women is demonstrated through this very intimate violation. A woman of colour has to process the same, but also, in majority-white countries, the shame of disclosing vulnerable details of a heinous act to a society that has historically sexualised and dehumanised her.

While unconscious bias may tell us that Black women are matriarchs, that they're tough and loud and can speak for themselves, we need to remind ourselves that people only display strength when they have no choice because of the challenges they face. And that display of strength doesn't necessarily reflect the humanity inside. It's not that some people are born with more fight in them – they're just forced to fight more.

Physical injuries will often heal after a sexual assault, but the feeling of degradation and helplessness stays. All survivors face this. But depending on their race, socioeconomic group or the circumstances of the attack, there may be more layers for some to unpick and process. I'm not ranking victimhood, just encouraging you to acknowledge that as much as you try, you may not be able to fully put yourself in someone else's shoes.

Were they asking for it?

I was once giving an interview on a Christian podcast when the interviewer asked me about sexual assault and rape. I don't know how we got there, but he'd had a discussion about the topic on a previous show and had received a number of calls – all from women – saying they believed women didn't help themselves and it was the responsibility of a woman to keep herself out of harm's way.

So here goes… We all have a responsibility to treat our bodies well; to care for our physical health and not take stupid risks, like crossing the road with our eyes closed. Women do take those precautions every day. They don't go running after dark, they walk home with their keys between their fingers, they message a friend to say they're home safely and they don't put their earphones in on the journey. But they shouldn't have to. If they didn't take these precautions and were attacked – *it wouldn't be their fault.*

A woman creating an opportunity for a man to attack her, by getting drunk, by walking alone at night or by separating from her friends, is not an excuse for crime. A woman making herself a desirable sexual partner by dressing up, flirting or generally being attractive is not an excuse for crime. A woman is *never* asking for it. Can we stop telling women 'Be good and you will be safe' and start telling men 'Be good and women will be safe'?

I believe we should teach girls and women how to defend themselves. In my first term of secondary school, we had a weekly self-defence class that did wonders for my confidence in handling scary situations. I still remember practising standing up and saying 'Can someone please help me? This man is exposing himself to me' in case I was ever caught by a flasher on the bus. I remember the advice that if you're worried you're being leered at, to overtly pick your nose to make yourself less appealing. I remember being told to shout 'Fire!' if I was ever being attacked, because people want to watch a fire, but no one wants to watch a rape. This is valuable and I'm grateful I learned it. But first and foremost, we should be teaching boys how to process their frustration in a healthy way, how to develop fruitful and nurturing relationships with girls, and that their masculinity isn't dependent on a woman's submission or sexual attention.

How many shades of grey?

I remember a university case a while back where a female student reported a male student for assault, but the charges were dropped after the police found amiable messages exchanged between them after the incident. This was seen as proof that she had consented to the sex and had no ill feelings after the event. I don't know the ins and outs of this story, so I can't comment on these decisions, but it's troubling that we place so much emphasis on messages like this.

I mentor women all the time who stayed in relationships after they were attacked. Some never even brought the incident up with their partner and carried on their normal dynamic straight after.

Some thought that if they could turn this violent encounter into a relationship, they could regain some control. Some thought that if they kept sleeping with the guy, they wouldn't be a slut who had one-night stands. In a lot of cases, it's only years down the line that a woman can finally use the word 'rape'.

In her book *Prey Tell*, Tiffany Bluhm cites many reasons why it may take a long time for a woman to come forward, including fear of retaliation, feelings of guilt and shame, and a desire to move on without the impending stress that is sure to accompany a public claim. She says: 'Years after their experiences, they struggle to grasp that what happened actually happened.'[8] While Shaila Dewan wrote for the *New York Times*: 'When the perpetrator is someone they trusted, it can take years for victims even to identify what happened to them as a violation.'[9]

At the very extreme and calculated end of the scale, there are whole message boards online with templates of texts men are urged to send to a woman the day after an assault, in order to protect themselves from prosecution. In her book *Men Who Hate Women*, Laura Bates writes:

> These messages specifically instruct men to send text messages the following day, designed to solicit responses that would weaken a woman's case if she tried to make an allegation of rape. Pressuring her to reply about the previous night, breezily referencing the great time had by all, doing everything that might coerce a traumatised victim into a placatory or ambivalent response.[10]

Tactics like this make it hard for people on the outside looking in to determine the actions and intentions of both the victim and the perpetrator. But you should know that there is no 'grey area' when it comes to sexual violence. Boys and men need to be taught the absolutes of consent so they are fully aware when they are crossing a line. And women need to fully understand their right to remove consent so they don't feel coerced into 'agreeing' to anything.

There are women who disagree with this. Writing for the *New York Times* in 1990, Camille Paglia rejected the idea that 'no means no'. She said, '"No" has always been, and always will be, part of the dangerous, alluring courtship ritual of sex and seduction, observable even in the animal kingdom.'[11]

While Katie Roiphe, again writing for the *New York Times*, said:

These feminists are endorsing their own utopian vision of sexual relations: sex without struggle, sex without power, sex without persuasion, sex without pursuit. If verbal coercion constitutes rape, then the word rape itself expands to include any kind of sex a woman experiences as negative.[12]

These women aren't wrong. Rejecting a man's advances with the purpose of increasing his longing and allowing him 'the thrill of the chase' is an engrained part of romance and seduction. But can we be better than that? We've seen the damage it causes, so if a woman wants to kiss someone, she shouldn't say no with the intention of making him work for it. This is only reinforcing the rhetoric that even women who say they don't want it actually do.

Crying wolf

Donald Trump said that the #MeToo movement, used to highlight the prevalence of sexual assault, made him more worried for his son than his daughter. This is a telling statement, but I'm not angry at him for it, because if people didn't voice their concerns honestly, we wouldn't be able to address them. Boys and men are worried that a night of fun could end up in a prison sentence, the loss of their job or expulsion from an educational facility. There are two elements to this: the first is that a man could have what he believes to be a consensual sexual interaction with someone and later find out that he is being accused of rape because it didn't, in fact, stand up against the criteria for enthusiastic, sober consent. Laura Bates cites TedX speaker Ben Hurst, who discusses fear among men and boys around accusations of rape. He suggests that a lot of their reaction to these conversations comes down to the fact that they are afraid – something they are encouraged to hide. Ben claims that men and boys often feel they can't admit to being scared they'll be accused of rape after a sexual encounter, so instead they just say that women lie about rape.[13]

Men can protect themselves against this by (a) strictly adhering to the guidelines I listed above without looking for any loopholes and without selfishly pursuing their own gratification; or (b) trying out the not-sleeping-with-people-till-marriage thing.

The second element is the concern that a man and woman truly did have completely consensual sex but the woman still 'cries rape' out of malice or regret, or for some other reason. Now, I don't want to deny that this happens, because it does, but it is incredibly rare. In *Men Who Hate Women*, Laura Bates explains that research shows: 'A man in the UK is 230 times more likely to be raped himself than be falsely accused of rape, so low is the number of false allegations.' In October 2018, Channel 4 conducted a detailed investigation into this phenomenon with the help of robust national statistics. It found that the average adult man in England and Wales has a 0.0002% chance of being falsely accused of rape in a year.[14]

When someone comes forward in church

Women who report sexual assault face huge challenges. In England and Wales in 2021, only 1 in 100 rapes reported to the police resulted in a charge – let alone a conviction.[15] This is deeply disappointing and damaging to the survivors of rape who reluctantly come forward. But in a church setting the stakes are even higher, as the response of the leadership can have an effect on that person's faith.

American lawyer Rachael Denhollander was the first to speak out about the abuse she suffered at the hands of USA Gymnastics team doctor Larry Nassar. She alleged that, instead of standing by her, her own church had been part of the cover-up and turned its back on her when she reported it. Her impact statement said: 'My advocacy for sexual assault victims, something I cherished, cost me my church and our closest friends three weeks before I filed my police report. I was left alone and isolated. And far worse, it was impacted because when I came out, my sexual assault was wielded like a weapon against me.'[16]

In *The Making of Biblical Womanhood*, Beth Allison Barr shares an example where former President of Southeastern Baptist Theological Seminary Paige Patterson advised an alleged rape survivor not to report the crime, but instead to forgive her rapist. She also highlights an incident where congregation member Jules Woodson wrote a blog about the sexual assault she had experienced aged seventeen, when celebrated pastor Andy Savage was her youth leader. A couple of weeks after the article went live, Pastor Andy stood up in front of his congregation at Highpoint Church in Memphis, Tennessee, and confessed to the assault he'd been accused of. He was greeted with a standing ovation for his honesty.[17]

For too long, women have been silenced or made to feel that they are 'ruining good men' by coming forward. Men who cover up assault are not good men. They made the choice to do something damaging. Truly repentant, good men would step forward without being backed into a corner, confess to their crime or misconduct, and accept the appropriate punishment or required amends from both the legal system and the Church.

Calling out toxic, coercive or abusive behaviour in another person is not an equal crime to that of the harmful behaviour itself.

It's not a crime *at all*, and a person who comes forward should be supported. It takes huge bravery. Sometimes these men have behaved in a coercive way but don't understand the gravity of their behaviour. It's just not a big deal to them. And it may not be… *to them*. But to someone else it can shatter their self-esteem and stay with them for life. It is very serious.

In her book, *Some Body to Love*, author Alexandra Heminsley tells how, while heavily pregnant, her bum was pinched on the train by a man who was part of a group that was behaving intimidatingly towards her. She reported this, and it went to court, but the magistrate refused to convict him because he said that being put on the sex offender's register would be too severe a punishment for the crime.[18] But that is the punishment for the crime – and if it doesn't fit, that's something the judicial system has to address, not something that should be borne by the victims of abuse.

This injustice is felt keenly by women who want to report a male leader's impropriety in the Church. In a job that relies on good standing in the community and high levels of accountability, a bad report could prove catastrophic. But that was the choice *he* made, not *her*.

Tiffany Bluhm says: 'We must be willing to talk about the atrocities that happen against women and make it plain that there is no room for such behavior, and that we will not sit silently while our sisters, mothers, and daughters endure unthinkable tragedy.'[19]

Women need to be given space to speak up about injustice in the Church. There needs to be a clear process for reporting, they need to be heard and they shouldn't be blamed for the disruption. Kat Armas says:

I always wonder why folks are so quick to think that speaking out against things like sexism, racism, abuse, homophobia, ableism, and such is more divisive than actually being sexist, racist, abusive, homophobic, or ableist. Speaking out against injustice isn't what divides – instead, acting in ways that are divisive does.[20]

Tiffany Bluhm advises: 'If an employee or church member comes forward with allegations, they must be informed that their voice matters, their allegations will be heard and investigated, and they will be supported.'[21]

Calling it out

Seven years ago I was invited to the launch of a new restaurant in the City of London. The banker-trap bar was teeming with suited professionals quaffing champagne and threatening to snort Colombia dry.

As I – then sober – shimmied around my handbag on the dancefloor with a few fellow PR girls, a group of blokes, easily twenty years our senior, sidled up to join us. The seemingly harmless guys cut stiff shapes while their gin and tonics lolloped out of their glasses, rendering the lacquered floor a slip hazard.

Then one swung his arm through the air and smacked my bum – hard. I turned around and surveyed the paunchy man with his shirt half untucked, and I felt embarrassed. Embarrassed for me and embarrassed for him. I left the dancefloor and went to the bar upstairs, then decided to leave the party altogether.

I've thought about that moment many times since and berated myself for not saying anything. I could have transferred my shame onto him by calling him out in front of his colleagues. Or I could even have asked security to intervene. I wanted to scream a shrill siren of distress, but I didn't. No one likes an over-reactor. I didn't want to – quite literally – be the butt of their jokes in the office on Monday morning. A year or so later, however, I got the chance to redeem myself.

I was out in Peckham for a friend's leaving do when one of his mates got three sheets to the wind and decided to slap my behind, once again on the dancefloor. I turned around and squared up to the man, whose girlfriend had left the event an hour previously, and said, 'Slap my arse again, and I'll slap your face.'

It was said sufficiently loudly to cause our fellow party-goers to stop and look with horrified expressions. I turned and immediately walked over to the bar, away from the group. I felt great, like Bridget Jones after publicly telling boss Daniel Cleaver where to shove his job before strutting out of the office. I had redeemed myself and struck a blow for women the world over. As I left, I imagined Aretha Franklin's 'Respect' blasting out through the speakers – the soundtrack to my triumph. The threat of violence wasn't ideal, although I'm 90% certain I wouldn't have actually hit him, but I felt so satisfied with myself that I decided, going forward, I would always call out toxic behaviour. Enough was enough.

I had my chance to put this into action a while later when a date took a dark turn. Everything was going well, and he invited me back to his place for dessert. I explained to my Christian date that I didn't want to sleep with him, but he insisted we could just watch a film. On arrival, I discovered he was crammed into a house share, where what used to be the living room had been converted into a bedroom.

With no communal space, I was forced to eat my ice cream sitting on his bedroom floor. He insisted I sit on his bed to watch a film, saying I shouldn't worry – he didn't bite – then proceeded to kiss me. I consented to this, but then he relentlessly tried to touch me as I said no, while continually having to move his hands off my legs, breasts and crotch.

Unsolicited grabbing is not usually physically painful, but I was instantly filled with dread. I knew that I could handle the act of intrusion in the moment, but I wondered how many years down the line I would still be thinking about it. I wondered how long it would take me to get over the emotional pain of being so disrespected and ignored. I said I was leaving, and he insisted on dropping me home. When I got out of the car and into the safety of my house, I pulled myself together and remembered the vow I had made. I left him a voice note explaining that I had said no, and I didn't feel that my wishes had been heeded.

He replied that, despite my verbal protestations: 'When we kissed you blew up like a f***ing firework!' I took one more stab at explaining the flaws in his logic. As a recovering cocaine addict, I might 'light up like a f***ing firework' if you rack up a line of coke in front of me. But I would say no to that too, and I wouldn't expect you to shove it up my nose because you believe you know what I want better than I do. He still didn't get it. I decided not to keep going. I had done my bit. I was not going to reason with rape culture. It was not my responsibility to educate him about consent. We didn't speak again.

I hadn't received the response I wanted, but I'd known it was unlikely. If he was the kind of person to ignore a 'no', he was hardly the kind to accept feedback and offer an unreserved apology. I hoped that spelled the end of my days confronting pushy men, and that my small contribution to the cause might have made one of those tiny differences that, teamed with hundreds of thousands of others, might lead to change.

Alas, it didn't turn out that way. I later met a man at a Christian event and we started dating. Everything was great initially, although he blurred the line between banter and cruelty. Then on our third date he grabbed my hand and put it on his penis. After this, I explained that I had no intention of having sex with him and asked him to stop.

He didn't. He also didn't stop with the taunting and teasing, and was rude about one of my close friends. We didn't work out. I didn't feel the need to rehash anything. He hadn't done anything against the law; he'd just been cavalier with my feelings and uncomfortably pushy when it came to physical intimacy. So, he went about his life and I went about mine, and we occasionally crossed paths but rarely spoke.

A few months later he phoned and told me he'd matched on a dating app with my friend, the one he'd been rude about, and wanted to check that I wouldn't object to them dating. I knew I needed to call him out. I felt fine with the idea of my mistreatment, but the suggestion that he could behave that way to someone I loved was unthinkable. Why do we always act more strongly to protect our friends than ourselves?

I explained that I wouldn't be able to report good experiences, when dating him had left me feeling insecure and as though I had little value. I also said I wouldn't hide his previous unkind comments about her. I got upset. He furiously accused me of misrepresenting the situation and said he didn't want to continue the conversation. The following day I got a message explaining the damage my suggestion of his misbehaviour had done to him. He disagreed with a lot of what I had said, and he accused me of being hurtful and aggressive. He said he didn't see any point going over it and wanted to draw a line there.

My resolve faltered. What if I was overreacting? Twisting things to fit my own victim narrative? What if it really wasn't that big a deal and I was being neurotic? What if the points I had raised *had* actually been forceful and aggressive, as he said? I asked myself the question thousands of Reddit users pose daily: 'Am I The A**hole'?

I mentor women all the time, and have never had a situation described to me where I've been unsure of fault or can't identify toxic behaviour, but in that moment I couldn't work it out. I have complete clarity about acceptable behaviour in every instance except the ones that involve myself. And the blindness leaves me unsure and frustrated.

I sought advice from a wise friend; a church leader whose job means she deals with pastorally difficult situations all the time. I told her in no uncertain terms to flag up when and where I was being 'the a**hole'. She validated my concerns and said how sorry she was that I had been treated in this way. I felt so relieved. On my suggestion, she agreed to mediate a sit-down with the two of us, where he could also bring a trusted and wise confidant from his church and we could all be heard safely. She thought it unlikely he'd agree.

She was right. He didn't agree. He blocked me.

By suggesting a sit-down with him and someone from his community, he said I was 'threatening' him. To him, this offer appeared more like a weapon than a recommended biblical response when two people can't agree.

The pain and panic of trying to explain how I felt to someone who was adamant I was wrong was too much to bear. To have my experiences denied when the cost of raising them had been so great was agonising. I felt empty, with fear, embarrassment and uncertainty echoing through me. I felt myself teetering dangerously close to the voice that says: 'Someone grabbing your bum is not a big deal – let it go, Lauren,' or, 'People touch you up when you're dating. This is just what happens – stop creating drama.'

Too many times I've felt as if I'm a case study for others' education; that people behave in a 'trial and error' way with me because they believe I have the strength to take it. I'm proud of any woman who decides to stand firm and call out this behaviour. But I never blame any woman who doesn't – it is agony.

Not long after this, I went to see *Prima Facie*, a one-woman West End play performed by Jodie Comer. In the fourth act, a victim says the words 'I have to find a way to want this' while she is being raped. The line kept replaying in my head, over and over. I think it is the most relatable thing I've heard. Many of us are terrified to stand before the mountain ahead of us in acknowledging – to ourselves, our families, the legal system and our churches – what has happened to us. So instead we try to find a way to want it. It is far easier to process a regrettable sexual experience than a rape. Far easier to be a slut than a victim.

A prayer

Lord God,

It feels as if there's no way back after a sexual assault. It's as if the person you were and the life you had is gone, and what you're left with will never be as good, light-hearted and joy-filled. I pray that you would show the path you have for each person reading this who feels broken. Not a path for them to go back to how they were before, but one for them to move forward into a new life, a new light, with a new sense of peace, wisdom and understanding. I pray for your hand of comfort to be on them. I pray that they can feel your arms around them.

I pray that you would give each person reading this your supernatural strength to be honest. To speak up and come forward, and let people know what they have been struggling to cope with in the dark on their own. I pray that it would be brought into the light. Whether that means confiding in a friend, a partner, a church leader or the authorities, I pray that you would lift the horrific fear of sharing something so personal and make it easier. I pray that you would prepare the person they speak to, so that they respond with love and kindness. That they would be able to listen and comfort and offer support.

I pray that you would speak truth over the lies of the enemy. I speak against shame or fear of judgement. I pray that each person reading this would know they didn't ask for this to happen to them. That they are worthy of so much more, and that another person's crime is not their responsibility. I pray that you would remove any low self-esteem or low self-worth and fill them with an overwhelming sense of your closeness. I pray that they would know they are deeply loved by their Father, the King, and that this would be the truth they walk in.

I thank you that we can fight back differently because we love you. We can bring our hurt and pain to you, and trust that you will fight for us. I pray that you would bring your incredible healing spirit into each person's life. That they won't be able to understand it – it is so deep and unexpected and profound and unlikely, that it can only be God. I pray that you would bless them as they walk with you.

I pray that your comfort would continue, even when the acute sting turns into a dull ache. I pray that you would still be there, ready to catch them, if something they thought they had dealt with rears its ugly head once again.

Please protect and walk with your sons and daughters as they pull close to you, despite the difficulties they have faced in this world. And we thank you for what you have waiting for us in the next.

Amen

Why Christians don't believe women who speak up

TIFFANY BLUHM

Tiffany Bluhm is the author of Prey Tell, Never Alone *and* She Dreams.

As a woman who is notorious for playing by the rules, I was mortified when I found myself in possession of information that could drastically change the lives of others. I so badly wanted to do the right thing, to speak up and tell the truth, but I knew beyond a shadow of a doubt that if I did, I wouldn't be heard. My voice, and the voices of other women, would be drowned out. Never mind that I, and the other women in my world, were devout followers of Jesus, had never been labelled as troublemakers or rabble rousers, and were in positions of leadership; still I knew that if we spoke truth to power, we would be silenced, subjugated and left to fight our own battles. Why? Because that's the way it's always been.

Despite women making up half the world, we are still stifled when we speak up against abuses of power. We see it in courtrooms, on the playground, in universities and, sadly, in sacred spaces. What should be the safest place for a woman to share the truth has often become a place of great pain. It takes strength and bravery to speak up as a truth-teller, and the sharp pain of not being heard can be a trauma in itself. As a society, as the Church, we must do better. Jesus modelled how.[1]

The belief that women are second-rate humans and unreliable with the truth was a prevalent one in the first century, when the early Church was finding its way. Jewish historian Flavius Josephus chronicles in his work *Antiquities of the Jews* why women should not be believed: 'But let not the testimony of women be admitted, on account of the levity and boldness of their sex... since it is probable that they may not speak truth, either out of hope of gain, or fear of punishment.'[2]

The idea that women aren't capable of telling the truth because they have some sort of agenda or competing interest, gain or fear has robbed women throughout history of being considered honest. Instead, we've been seen as bodies to be dominated and voices to be silenced. This is evidenced by the way the Church has painted women throughout history as 'corrupt' or, my personal favourite, 'the devil's gateway' – a phrase coined by early Church father Tertullian. If women were stereotyped as untrustworthy, they could be easily dismissed and passed over. Yet throughout Scripture we see the value of listening to women, crescendoing with Jesus entrusting the message of the resurrection to a woman who knew him well.

During the first century in Greco-Roman culture, women had the same status as slaves, with their value coming through their ability to bear children and carry on a family line. This is a far cry from how we treat women today, yet the belief that a woman's role is to stay quiet and take care of children still remains in the culture of some churches across the developing and developed world. Many Christian denominations equate quiet women with holiness; that if a woman is submissive and quiet, it means she's spiritually mature. However, a closer look at the gospel, not through a patriarchal lens but rather through the lens of justice, offers a robust understanding of women as equal – to be seen and also *heard* as equals.

In my previous work exploring how we treat women when they speak up, I wrote:

Scripture exemplifies the importance and necessity of believing women as it has radically altered individual lives, like that of

Naaman, a respected army commander who believes his wife's young Israelite slave girl, who tells him he should visit the prophet in Samaria to find healing from his leprosy, and indeed he finds the relief he's longed for when he does what the little girl has proposed (2 Kings 5:1–19). Believing women changes not only individual lives but also the course of history for an entire people group. In the book of Esther, a Jewish teen who becomes queen of an ancient empire is believed by her king when she confesses that his chief counsel has planned to annihilate her people. Because she is believed, she saves an entire race from mass genocide (Esther 7). Later, in the first century, Jesus defied the judicial, civil, and religious practices that treated women as second in society. To him, they were equals with men, and their voice held weight. His actions challenged the cultural position that women's testimonies were untrustworthy, despite the common beliefs of his time.[3]

We would also be wise to remember the bravery of the woman at the well who ran back to her village after a life-altering chat with Jesus, and spoke to anyone who would listen about the man who knew all the details of her life. They heeded her call and were introduced to their Messiah (John 4:28–30, 39–42). Mary Magdalene, a woman who financed the work of the ministry of Jesus, and had been healed of demons, was 'an apostle to the apostles': she, rather than Peter or John, announced Christ's resurrection to the rest of the disciples. An entire faith rests on the testimony of a woman who witnessed a very dead man come to life and address her by name. Jesus emphatically valued a woman's voice; so much so that he left the mantle of proclamation to none other than the 'lesser' sex.

Refusing to silence or label a woman's voice as needy, clingy, emotional, dramatic or angry takes practice, because nearly all of us, in one space or another, have been culturally conditioned to see women as such. But if we long to lean in to the coming kingdom, we must break our bad habit of judgements – including assuming that if something unfortunate happens to a woman she must have done something to deserve it. We must listen and learn, not convince ourselves we would handle things better under pressure than she did. A woman's voice is to be respected, heard and valued, and as we do these things we'll witness the growth and empowerment of all God's children.

Righteous anger

Warning: this chapter contains details of violence and sexual violence.

It's when I hear about pictures of young girls circulating on the internet. It's when someone is forced to testify in court, eye to eye with their rapist, and justify every sexual decision they ever made. It's when someone makes a joke at another person's expense, knowing they don't have the capacity or ability to push back with equal force. It's any attempt to belittle someone through humiliation. It's the exertion of power and physical strength over someone who is not physically your equal. It's the selfish extraction of personal pleasure from a person who will spend the rest of their life paying the price for it.

It's a sick feeling in my stomach and a buzzing in my head. It's every husband or wife who has been made to feel crazy by a partner. It's the recurring clip playing over and over in my mind that I can't unsee. It's every woman who thinks that, although the world may say she was raped, she's not a victim because she was asking for it. It's the tears that well up in my eyes and the lump in my throat I have to swallow down.

It's every man who's called me fat or accused me of being a child for not wanting to have sex with him. It's every bloke who's grabbed me on a dancefloor, or worse. I know that I can take it; I've been forced to develop a skin thicker than I would have wished for.

I look at my friends' children or I help out on the school run, and I see those little girls I love and care about, and want to hold close and protect. If one of them went out and never came home; if they said no and no one listened; if they tried to defend themselves but they didn't have the strength... I would set fire to this whole place and watch it burn.

I remember the craze for 'happy slapping' when I was a teenager. Kids with new camera phones started punching people in the face on the street and sending the videos to each other. I wasn't a Christian then, but it made me feel physically sick. It wasn't the pain of the slap; it was the humiliation caused by having your trauma triumphantly circulated to others. I saw a gang of lads do it to a man in his thirties at Clapham Junction. I watched as an old woman stooped down to pick up his glasses from the floor and ask if he was okay. It felt like my first brush with pure devil-driven evil. I was too young to feel the anger I should have then. I just felt scared and upset and disgusted as these eighteen-year-olds dashed down the street asking one another to Bluetooth them the clip. Back then there were so few viral videos that everyone knew the latest one.

I remember when I first watched one of the videos for myself. I still think about it to this day. A girl of fifteen walked down the stairwell in an estate and was stopped by a group of teenagers about her age, boys and girls. I don't know where this was, but their accents suggested London. They questioned her about money and she said she didn't have anything, so the two girls started beating her up. They didn't just punch her in the stomach or the face. She was held down while others inflicted pain on her, all filmed by one of the boys, who cheered and egged the others on. When they were finished, they picked her up by her hair so that the camera got a clear view of her battered face, then they sent her running down the stairs.

I wasn't shown this at church, but I was shown it by an older Christian boy I knew from church. I was so distraught that I told my mum, who told him he couldn't come into our house again with his phone if that sort of thing was going to be on it. I cried about it a lot. I remember speaking to my sister. She was a Christian, and she told me that this was one of the reasons her faith was so important to her. She said the burden of justice wasn't on her. I remember her exact wording: 'They will get theirs.' Whether in this life or the next, no one gets away without answering for their sins – but that's not our job; it's God's.

I didn't know what I believed then, but I do now. Maybe this is an area for growth in my Christian journey, but I do hope they get theirs. I hope they experience more pain than they inflicted on that girl. I hope someone explains to them exactly why they have to experience it.

I know that God feels this pain. But when it really matters, do I trust his justice? Do I want a fair trial? Do I want compassion, grace and kindness? Or do I want retribution? Do I want disproportionate pain? Do I want to see people feel as small as they made others feel? Am I scared that if I leave it to God he will show too much mercy?

'And forgive us our trespasses, as we forgive those who trespass against us.' But I never did what they did. I never pushed the bounds of forgiveness to that extreme; never raped or caused GBH; never enjoyed and promoted another person's humiliation.

I have done wrong. I have bullied. I have belittled. I have promoted myself. I have harmed myself more times than I can count. But I'm different now. Should they get to be different now? Do they get to repent and walk away? Do they get freedom from their sin when others still live in the shadow of it?

I'm angry, and I know that it goes beyond the point of righteous anger. I know I need to pedal back – and I will in time. It's anger that prompts change, but I can't be positive until I learn to forgive. And that means facing the pain. It means talking about the places where it hurts. It means letting friends and mentors and confidants see. It means being honest about it, instead of letting it fester inside me for twenty years. There are some things I've gripped on to so tightly that I've allowed my resentment to become part of my identity. I want to hand all of that pain and anger to God, instead of desperately wanting to force it onto others. I don't want hatred.

I want to absorb my pain without passing it on. I know that's what Jesus did. They tried to break him. They did everything possible to harm and humiliate him. They beat him. They stripped him of his clothes. They held him up on the cross so everyone could see his agony. But his capacity to absorb pain was greater than their ability to inflict it. He never wavered. He asked God to forgive them. He offered excuses for their behaviour. He defended them. He answered their hatred with love.

This is true power, this is true strength, and I don't know if I'll ever get there. In my darkest moments I don't want to get there. But I will start with prayer. I will pray for the supernatural healing of victims, that they – especially that young girl – are living faith-filled lives beyond their wildest dreams. I will pray that the perpetrators never inflict pain like that again. I will pray for the protection of those I love.

I will submit my idea of justice to God. I will pray for a deeper faith and trust in his will and judgement. I will believe him when he says that his justice will roll like a river. I will pray that my heart aligns with Jesus', that I will be able to take what is thrown at me and only ever give back love. I will pray that I can forgive those who do horrendous things. And when I don't feel like I want any of that, I will pray for the will to want it – because sometimes that's where I have to start.

What Christians (men and women) can do next

Women

I've prayed a couple of formative but challenging prayers in my life. I once got down on my knees and prayed that God would develop in me a deep patience and perseverance. Do you know what would have been better? If God had just given me all the good things straight away, so I was never in need of great patience. That prayer was the rookiest of all rookie errors. I now have much more patience, because he has relentlessly given me things to wait for. I don't know if I'm grateful or resentful, but I do recognise the benefits.

The other reckless prayer I prayed was asking God to 'break my heart for what breaks yours'. I wanted to know what really hurt God; I wanted a glimpse of the world through his eyes. I believe he gave me a tiny glimpse. I can't handle all the heartbreak God deals with, and I know that I do things that break his heart. But I started to feel actual pain when I saw women being poorly treated, especially when it involved sexual violence and rape. I began to feel uncontrollably angry.

In *The Moment of Lift*, Melinda Gates writes: 'The lesson I've learned from women in social movements all over the world is that to bring about a revolution of the heart, you have to let your heart break. Letting your heart break means sinking into the pain that's underneath the anger.'[1] I would encourage you to let your heart break, to face the pain of it and to channel that into positive and loving action.

I don't care if you prefer not to use the word 'feminism', but please support women who continue to push forward for greater equality and freedoms. None of us will ever fully understand the sacrifices other women have made to help us have the opportunities we do now – all the way from the Bible to the suffragettes, to those carving out positive change today.

Don't let your disagreement with some areas of the feminist movement prevent you from seeing the vast beauty of the collective battles that have been won. Don't let people you think of as being too radical ruin it for you. Take the time to discern the difference between what is extreme and what is inherently God-ordained and good.

If you haven't experienced some of the hardships we've looked at, then that is truly great. But this may be because someone else went through them for you. Don't let the fact that your personal experience isn't aligned with others' prevent you from empathising, particularly with those from other socioeconomic groups and ethnicities. You may think you know their journeys, but I promise you don't. Let's all listen to each other. If something is not available to all of us, we're not done.

For people who feel the weight of this most heavily, let's pray for God's comfort. Let's pray for women who've walked out of church because they feel so let down by the leadership, or even the other women who don't speak up to support them. Check in on them, listen to them, cover them in prayer. Stand side by side with them.

And finally, don't blindly make my opinions, or the opinions of anyone referenced in this book, your opinions. Take each of these topics and pray about them, read Scripture and a range of commentaries, and consult your church leaders. This isn't a reference book for your new position on contentious topics; it's the start of the conversation.

Men (in addition to all of the above)

I get that some of the men reading this won't like the word 'feminism'. If you don't want to use it, then don't. But if you disagree with the fundamental principles, I think you really should delve deeper and chat to your church leader about it.

I understand if you don't agree with me about male headship in the home, but we can at the very least agree that the power afforded to men has been the source of an immeasurable amount of evil in the world. We all need to tread carefully when it comes to navigating power and leadership. As Franciscan priest Richard Rohr says: 'Only love can safely handle power.'[2]

I get it – sexist jokes can be funny. I can't think of any right now, but I'm sure there are a couple out there. Playing on stereotypes is a well-worn path for comedic acclaim, so if you prefer tired tropes to creativity and innovation, then who am I to criticise? But please know that every sexist comment, every objectification, every time you underestimate someone because they're a woman, you're creating a platform from which far worse misogynistic crimes can stand. You're not evil (probably), but your small participation could affirm the direction of someone else who is moving towards evil. That's why it matters. Not because we're oversensitive or can't take a joke. But because you, the 'not all men' men, aren't the ones who see the domestic violence and sexual assault inflicted by the men you unwittingly affirm.

Parents and teachers

You know when your ninety-year-old granny makes a horrific comment at the TV and you have to weigh up whether or not to correct her and ruin Christmas Day for everyone, or let it slide because she won't be around for much longer? That is never a question when it comes to children – always correct them.

Parents should be aware of what they model to their children, because no matter what words parents share, it's the family dynamic that children will remember. Don't be upset if, when they grow up, they land in a different place on some biblical issues around women.

Be excited that they have taken the time to explore and wrestle with it themselves, and trust that God will iron out any issues, for all of you.

Don't just teach children abstinence from sex before marriage. Yes, do teach them the physical, emotional and spiritual benefits of waiting until marriage, but if that's all you tell them, you'll let them down. The fact is, a huge number of Christians will not adhere to this; some will plan to and then fall short, and some won't have planned to at all. You also need to teach them about consent, and not just a muffled 'yes' after twenty 'no's, but enthusiastic, sober consent on both sides as an absolute prerequisite for any intimate contact. This protects them from unwittingly pushing for something their partner doesn't want, and protects their partner from finding him or herself in a horrific situation.

Educators and anyone in a position of influence in a child's life need to pull together with parents to make sure boys and girls are well rounded, supportive and respectful of one another. Campaigner Laura Bates has found that when speaking in schools, she gets an infinitely better response from mixed groups when she asks pupils to sit in a boy-girl-boy-girl formation, as the boys are 'stripped of bravado' when they can't move as a pack.[3]

Keep your children off the internet for as long as possible – and when they do go on it, know that it's not just 'adult' sites you need to block. YouTube is designed in a way that allows people to fall deeper and deeper down a rabbit hole. A child can start by watching a funny video compilation of football gaffes and be slowly nudged towards more extreme ideas and content. It's tactics like this that are used by the incel community to recruit new members to their woman-hating movement.

If you can see that a child is becoming increasingly extreme in their views and starting to engage more with a negative rhetoric around women, have an open conversation about it. Often teenagers get caught up in these groups because they feel isolated and alone.

It gives them a community to be a part of. If that's the case, the best thing you can do is give them a new gang to join. Help them explore different team sports, maybe get them into a boxing club. Take them to a club centred around a hobby, or introduce them to people of their own age at a church. Help them to find people who love and accept them, but within a healthy environment. That's the tactic the bad guys use, so why not turn it against them? Believe me, it works.

At work

In *The Authority Gap*, Mary Ann Sieghart writes:

It's as if men are swimming with the current in a river and women are swimming against it. The men see the banks racing past them and congratulate themselves for swimming so powerfully. They look at the women struggling to make headway against the current and think, 'Why can't they swim as fast as me? They're obviously not as good.'[4]

I know there's a feeling among some men that they are attacked for being successful at work, when in reality they're just better. They feel sorry that there isn't as much diversity at the top, but what can they do when the white men like them are genuinely the best and most qualified at the job? When opportunities aren't equal, there's no way of knowing whether abilities are equal.

Katherine W. Phillips, former Professor of Organizational Character at Columbia University's Business School, journalist Emily Bazelon shared how she was in a meeting with a group of managing directors at a New York bank. The group asked her: 'How do you explain to the white man with equivalent qualifications to a woman or a person of color the decision to hire or promote them instead of him?' Her response was: 'Well, what do you say to the woman or person of color who was equally capable? Why do you assume that the position belonged to the white man?'[5]

There is bias in all of us. Sometimes we're aware of it, but more often than not we don't have a clue. There's no need to wallow in shame about it. Acknowledge it and pray that every time you operate from a place of bias, God flags it so you can be aware and make changes accordingly.

If you're in a position of influence or leadership, don't use it to exclude. The first thing you need to do is be great at your own job. Feel secure in it, know that you're adding value, accumulate skills you can pass on, and feel enthusiastic about the role. People who feel welcome are able to extend a welcome to others. Don't allow yourself to feel threatened by others in your industry. Do your job well and encourage others to do the same.

If you're in a position to hire people, make sure there are at least two women on a selection panel or, if you're a man and it's a smaller organisation, that you've consulted women in the process. According to Mary Ann Sieghart:

> Having only one [woman involved in the process] decreases the chance of a woman being hired. That is because the men think that they don't have to worry about diversity; they can delegate it to the woman. And the woman fears that if she champions a female candidate, the men will think that she is being nepotistic.[6]

Next, remember that one woman's failure isn't all women's failure. We see this all the time with positions of power. If a woman gets the job and does it badly, there's a feeling that women just aren't up to the task. Whereas you would never conclude that men aren't good at a role just because one performed poorly.

You can make a real effort to ensure that your work environment is accommodating for mothers to return from maternity leave or after a number of years out caring for children. There are loads of mums who are working in jobs they are vastly overqualified for because they need flexibility to care for their family. I have a friend who says that the mothers he employs are the most valuable untapped resource and bring a huge amount of talent to his organisation. All he has to do is be flexible when they say they have to clock off for a couple of hours or when they need to prioritise their children.

And finally, if you're a bloke, don't talk over women. Give them the space to communicate their ideas, and be aware that there can be a tendency to interrupt them in corporate settings. Handing over airtime when you can see that it's not being offered is important.

Church

Before I say what follows, I should make it clear that I love the Church and it gets so much right. I don't envy the job of church leaders and am delighted to have been discipled by so many incredible ones – men and women. Lots of women in British churches feel honoured, respected and heard.

In a recent survey involving 800 women, *Premier Christianity* reported that more than half of respondents saw the biblical teaching on women as culture-specific, and nearly 70% disagreed with the statement: 'Women should not be in authority over men in church leadership.' A whopping 90% agreed that the gospel liberates women to be themselves, and more than three-quarters said that women's voices were not stifled in their church.[7] This is great news, but it does leave a quarter of women still feeling unheard, and that needs to be addressed.

The sad fact is, to many non-Christians, the Church is synonymous with misogyny and bigotry. I've heard people use Christianity as an explanation for hate speech. The conversation usually goes:

'And then he/she said [insert very sexist thing here].'

'Erm, what?! How can they actually think that?!'

'Yeah, I know. They're just one of those proper hardcore Christians.'

'Oh, right. That makes sense.'

A lot of the world only sees Christianity through the eyes of Louis Theroux or Netflix exposés. And a lot of the world thinks we live under a hierarchy of suppression. A 2015 *HuffPost* article on right-wing Christianity said: 'The faster conservative religion is overwhelmingly seen as mean, crazy, violent, hateful, misogynistic and anti-science, the faster we as a society can move on.'[8]

In *Abuelita Faith*, Kat Armas says that the symbol of the cross 'has historically been used as a weapon of hate, pain, and oppression'.[9] Former US president Jimmy Carter said that he believed the abuse of women and girls was 'the most serious and unaddressed worldwide challenge', and he thought the principal blame for it lay in the false interpretation of Scripture.[10]

If Jesus hadn't risen from his grave, he'd be turning in it.

The Church has got to do better. In society, it's often simplest to blame one individual for their behaviour, while singling out a whole group of people is seen as extreme. But Kat Armas explains that not acknowledging a fault with a system means we all play a part in upholding it and are therefore accountable.

We need to ask ourselves why we do things and why our traditions are in place. 'Because we've always done it that way' won't fly any more. The most successful organisations and people are those who adapt and grow, and don't resist change. That's not to say we should update Scripture to reflect the current societal tide, but we should be open to the idea that not all of our practices are based on Scripture. Some could just be a hangover from the imperfect practices of previous societies and times. Melinda Gates says: 'The purpose of conversations about old practices [is] to take out bias and add in empathy.'[11] So maybe it's time we started doing that.

The Church can do more to lift women up. Some churches already do this excellently. They may have a couple of blind spots that will get ironed out in time, but everything in life is progress, not perfection. Some churches, however, are letting down half their congregations. This is felt particularly acutely by single women. We need to do more to make sure women don't feel inferior if they aren't attached to a man. The Church is, generally speaking, terrible at this. For more info, you can check out my other book, *Notes on Love*.[12]

We need to challenge the Church to stop shying away from speaking about sex, women's bodies and women's pleasure. For years, Christians have felt deep shame around 'sinful' sex. We don't often hear people say how great sex can be and what an incredible God-given creation it is, when experienced at the right time. Christy Bauman says:

> I want to understand how I can know God through my feminine body. God was not uncertain when he made a woman's body and her reproductive and sexual organs. If a woman is to know salvation through childbearing, I believe salvation is also to be studied and known through the understanding of the woman's womb and reproductive system.[13]

This isn't embarrassing or shameful teaching, and it needs to be spoken about.

Churches would benefit from having more women in positions of influence and leadership – and not just via their husbands. Their representation will make an impact on congregations and mean that church decisions are considered from the perspective of more of the people they affect. Tokenism should be avoided, of course, but when I asked the All Saints focus group about the best way to do this, the answer was clear. If we look around the room and pick the one Black woman to stand at the front and do the notices, this is tokenism. We need to look around the room and identify people who classically wouldn't have been given the opportunity to speak in church, and then take the time to get to know them, to find out what their passions are, what their God-given talent is. Then we nurture them and help them to step into their calling, and invite them to showcase the unique skills God has given them when representing the Church. Having someone on stage should be the visible fruit of the deep roots they have grown through your leadership, time and investment. That's how it stops being tokenism.

God listens to the cries of women and he acts, so the Church should too. Time and time again, the Bible shows us that God lives most powerfully in the most powerless. Beth Allison Barr says: 'The harshest words Jesus utters in the Bible are to the strict male religious leaders functioning as self-appointed border guards of orthodoxy.'[14] Look at Matthew 23:27, where Jesus says: 'Woe to you, teachers of the law and Pharisees, you hypocrites! You are like whitewashed tombs, which look beautiful on the outside but on the inside are full of the bones of the dead and everything unclean.' Let's all examine our hearts and make sure we are working with God to do his will, and not working against it.

A litany to honor women

We walk in the company of the women who have gone
    before, mothers of the faith both named and unnamed,
testifying with ferocity and faith to the Spirit of wisdom and
    healing. They are the judges, the prophets, the martyrs,
    the warriors, poets, lovers, and saints
who are near to us in the shadow of awareness, in the
    crevices of memory, in the landscape of our dreams.

We walk in the company of Deborah,
who judged the Israelites with authority and strength.

We walk in the company of Esther,
who used her position as queen to ensure the welfare of her
    people.

We walk in the company of you whose names have been
    lost and silenced,
who kept and cradled the wisdom of the ages.

We walk in the company of the woman with the flow of
    blood,
who audaciously sought her healing and release.

We walk in the company of Mary Magdalene,
who wept at the empty tomb until the risen Christ appeared.

We walk in the company of Phoebe,
who led an early church in the empire of Rome.

We walk in the company of **Perpetua of Carthage,**
whose witness in the third century led to her martyrdom.

We walk in the company of **St. Christina the Astonishing,**
who resisted death with persistence and wonder.

We walk in the company of **Julian of Norwich,**
who wed imagination and theology, proclaiming, 'All shall
be well.'

We walk in the company of **Sojourner Truth,**
who stood against oppression, righteously declaring in 1852,
'Ain't I a woman!'

We walk in the company of **the Argentine mothers of the
Plaza de Mayo,**
who turned their grief to strength, standing together to
remember 'the disappeared' children of war with a holy
indignation.

We walk in the company of **Alice Walker,**
who named the lavender hue of womanish strength.

We walk in the company of you mothers of the faith,
who teach us to resist evil with boldness, to lead with
wisdom, and to heal.

Amen.[1]

And finally...

Queen Elizabeth II was an excellent driver, and during the war she was a mechanic. But as the most senior monarch, she had a chauffeur who did virtually all her driving for her. In 1998, then-Crown Prince Abdullah of Saudi Arabia visited Balmoral Castle and, much to his surprise, the Queen insisted she would drive him herself. At the time, all women in Saudi Arabia, royal or otherwise, were banned from driving.

Women are capable, hilarious, intelligent, passionate and faithful. We are surrounded by examples of this every day. But not everyone sees it. In his 1920 book, *Our Women*, Arnold Bennett tackled the question 'Are men superior to women?' His answer was: 'The truth is that intellectually and creatively man is the superior of woman, and that in the region of creative intellect there are things which men almost habitually do but which women have not done and give practically no sign of ever being able to do.'[1]

Yes, this was a hundred years ago, but we still live in the shadow of that popular opinion. And the Church is sadly not where it could be when it comes to restoring the dignity of women. I truly believe that Christianity can liberate women and give them a voice, but in many ways our cultural interpretations take that away. Beth Allison Barr says:

> We are called to be different from the world. Yet in our treatment of women, we often look just like everyone else. Ironically, complementarian theology claims it is defending a plain and natural interpretation of the Bible while really defending an interpretation that has been corrupted by our sinful human drive to dominate others and build hierarchies

of power and oppression. I can't think of anything less Christlike than hierarchies like these.[2]

Although they are a point of great pride for Christians, it's okay for us to review some of our traditions. Some of our historical practices have been taken out of the hands of good, God-focused people and used to push women down. Women are called to obedience – not to men, but to God. And the same goes for men. A woman's place is not under the power of a man; it's under the power of God. Aimee Byrd says:

> If we are in union with Christ, then our house is full indeed. When we go to the riches in his Word, we don't find a masculine and a feminine version, but one Bible to guide us all. We don't find that our ultimate goal is biblical manhood or biblical womanhood but complete, glorified resurrection to live eternally with our Lord and Savior Jesus Christ.[3]

In Jesus, we have a role model who didn't rigidly stick to the religion of his day. He recognised the intention behind the rules and saw that some were obsolete, some weren't, and some could be adapted or implemented differently. I understand wanting to cling to rules. When I first went into recovery I followed every 'rule' I was given. I didn't allow myself an inch of interpretation because I knew that if I did, I was liable to abuse it. But as I've grown in my recovery, I can see that it's not a one-size-fits-all situation and that, while they may have been helpful initially, some of the rules I was given are no longer helpful or fruitful. For example, I went to a support group every day for my first ninety days. That rigidity was important to me when I was newly sober. But now that I understand myself and have greater maturity in my recovery, I don't feel the need to maintain that routine.

We cling to the rules because the spirit of the rules is so much harder to interpret and live out. Sometimes it's dangerous to give people license to explore and make their own minds up, but that's the freedom Jesus gave us. And it's patronising to assume that only some people can hear God, develop a close relationship with him and follow where he's leading.

Jesus was spectacular at turning hierarchy on its head and celebrating those who were forgotten or cast aside. We need to be, too. If you're a person who feels discarded in or out of the Church, I'm sorry. We all need to do better. In the words of Beth Allison Barr: 'Jesus set women free a long time ago. Isn't it finally time for evangelical Christians to do the same?'

You may not agree with me and, as I said in the beginning, I expect that even if you do broadly, you won't agree with everything. That's okay. That doesn't mean you or I are discounted from the conversation. People who don't believe what you believe aren't stupid or uneducated. They just believe something different. As long as we're not venturing into the realms of extremism, respect for people's principles has to underpin these discussions.

Everyone is free to research more, learn more and change their mind. That's what's so exciting about growth. But we need to put our relationships before the disagreement. The devil doesn't need to trick us all into either inviting women on stage or not inviting women on stage. He just needs to get us fighting about it.

Rachel Held Evans, who very sadly passed away a few years after *A Year of Biblical Womanhood* was published, says:

There are some women who wrestle with the rules, some who uncritically accept the rules, and some who thrive within the rules. There are those who flourish under the creative constraints of tradition, and those who struggle to find their voice. There are women for whom the bonnets and aprons foster humility and women for whom the same things foster pride.[4]

I have a deep respect for anyone who wrestles with this and lands in a place of love, no matter how that plays out in their life. But I do feel upset when women aren't empowered to make that decision and are pushed into a complementarian arrangement without being given a chance to work out what they believe.

Women – you don't have to have what the world says is 'it all'. If you have what God has called you to, you already have 'it all'. For some that will be working for a charity, for some that will be two beautiful children, for some that will be a power suit and an office, and for some that will be church ministry.

But let's also remember that not all women have the luxury of 'chasing their calling'. For some, staying at home with children isn't an option. Quoting Patrick Reyes, Kat Armas says: 'God often just calls us to survive.' She adds: 'This is true for most people in the world; their Christian "calling" is simply survival. But this, too, is a holy, sacred endeavor.'[5]

Ultimately, women have been made to feel that they need to ask permission to speak: in church, in the boardroom and sometimes at home. But that's just not the case. They have a valuable and necessary input to share with the world, and must be given the space to share it.

When you include people who have previously been excluded from a decision-making process, everyone benefits. Everyone gets a boost from including women. Mary Ann Sieghart dispels the preconception that gender equality works on the same principle as a seesaw. Increased support for one gender does not mean that the other is denigrated. Instead, we are all better off when men and women are treated equally.[6]

Ultimately every person should be given the dignity they deserve in Christ. Every single one of us, regardless of gender, is made in God's image. We are designed to be relationally close and to live in community. If we all prioritised the first- and second-most important commandments: 'Love the Lord your God with all your heart and with all your soul and with all your mind' and 'Love your neighbour as yourself', we would find most of these debates and conversations completely redundant.

It's not about men versus women. It's about Christians being *for* everyone. It's about having heavenly eyes open to seeing injustice and God-given strength to stand up against it. Let's lift each other up. And let's leave no man *or woman* behind.

PS: Don't forget we agreed you'd message someone and ask them to pray for you when you finished the book. It's now time.

Acknowledgements

Always God first. God gave me the idea, opportunity and words for this project. He put the right people in my path to discuss the topics and the right team to bring the book to life. I am so proud to start, end and live my days with the wisdom, strength and comfort of God as my guide.

Next, my family: there are two whole new little people in my life since the last book, and taking 'baby Jesse breaks' and anticipating the arrival of my new niece or nephew really kept me going through the writing process. My obsession with Leo and Inez continues to grow, and they are an unending source of joy. Thanks to Cathie, who read the first chapter of this and assured me it wasn't total rubbish. To Nathan for reading what I assume will be his first and last book on feminism. To Dad for always wanting to hear how my work's going, being my career counsellor and offering me a Devon sanctuary for when it gets too much.

To Mum, who has seen my faith continue to grow but, through this book, had to allow my opinions to diverge from her own. Thank you for helping me to explore and for continually bringing me back to the Bible as my guide.

Rosie. Rosie, Rosie, Rosie, Rosie… the first person to get excited about this book. The first person to pray about it and keep praying for the following two years. My encourager and champion and confidante. Thank you so much for the way you've held my arms up when I was too weak to do it myself.

Thank you to the women I love and trust who have supported me in prayer, with fasting, with songs, with kind words and love: Jo, Caroline, Clare, Kirky, Tiff, Claire, Laura, Lizzie, Rosie G, Charlotte, Lucy, Ali, Becs, Holly and Emma. And also to my friends who don't believe this stuff, but know it is of central significance to my life and deeply respect that: Tess, Emma, Alex, Harri and Louise.

I am lucky to have incredible male friends. Not just ones you only keep around because you sort of fancy them and hope they will ask you out, but real, genuine friendships with people who will move heaven and earth to support you. Or at least stay up assembling flat-pack furniture with you till 1 a.m. Sam – my favourite feminist and breeze chatter – I have no humour without our memes and ridiculous quotes. Alex – send more Taytos. Barney – for finally acknowledging that I'm not just funny 'for a girl'.

To each person who shared their views with me and got involved in discussions on feminism and faith to benefit this book, I am so grateful. A special thanks goes to the sisters of the Community of Our Lady of Walsingham and to those who attended one of the focus groups: Meriel, Lois, Indi, Amie, Jen, Holly, Michelle, George, Nick, Sam and Paul. And in particular Katie and Lois, who both read through the manuscript to give their frank perspectives on its content – including cutting out some of the weaker jokes.

To Dave, whom everyone thought I forgot to acknowledge in *Notes on Love* because I jiggled the names around and renamed him David. The other guys in Foo Fighters may have laughed at you – but who's laughing now?

Thank you to Elizabeth Neep, a woman I genuinely believe I could take over the world with if she'd just give up publishing and start co-leading the coup. But for now, I will settle for having her as my editor – she makes every book I attempt better with her wise feedback and invaluable experience. A huge thanks must also go to Katherine Venn, another titan of Christian publishing, whose thoughtful notes and edits elevated the book no end. I consider it a personal favour from God that you were temporarily involved in the project.

Thanks also to Joy Tibbs. I love that my project editor is someone whose own writing is so uplifting and makes me laugh so much.

This book is greatly improved thanks to your diligence. Plus, the whole team at SPCK who worked so hard to make this book great and to ensure that others knew about it.

And finally, to everyone who reads this book or *Notes on Love*. Anyone who follows me on social media and responds to my weird Q&As on stories. Anyone who's signed up to my newsletter. Anyone who's ever emailed or DM-ed me about the book or my sobriety or, even better, *their* sobriety. Thank you a million times over. Life's more fun when we do it together, and like-minded, good-humoured Christians are my absolute favourite. Let's keep opening our arms and widening the circle: the more the merrier.

Notes

Introduction

1 'Women in Ministry – Dr. Sandra Richter', Asbury Theological Seminary, 5 March 2018: https://www.youtube.com/watch?v=tpmtq-ZsqC4 (accessed 18 October 2023).

2 Given, F., *Women Don't Owe You Pretty* (London: Cassell, 2020).

The 'F' word

1 'The Danvers Statement', Council on Biblical Manhood and Womanhood, November 1988: https://cbmw.org/about/danvers-statement (accessed 19 December 2023).

2 'The Tenets of Biblical Patriarchy', Vision Forum Ministries: https://web.archive.org/web/20110423132323/http://www. visionforumministries.org/home/about/biblical_patriarchy.aspx (accessed 19 December 2023).

3 Chancey, J. and McDonald, S., *Passionate Housewives Desperate for God: Fresh vision for the hopeful homemaker* (San Antonio, TX: The Vision Forum, 2007).

4 Clinton, T. and Davis, M., *Take It Back: Reclaiming biblical manhood for the sake of marriage, family and culture* (Lake Mary, FL: Charisma House, 2021).

5 Piper, J. and Grudem, W. A., *Recovering Biblical Manhood & Womanhood: A response to evangelical feminism* (Wheaton, IL: Crossway, 2021).

6 Byrd, A., *Recovering from Biblical Manhood & Womanhood: How the Church needs to rediscover her purpose* (Grand Rapids, MI: Zondervan, 2020), pp. 104–06.

7 Solanas, V., 'S.C.U.M. (Society for Cutting Up Men) Manifesto', (London: Olympia Press, 1968).

8 Greer, G., *The Female Eunuch* (London: MacGibbon & Kee, 1970).

9 Sommers, C. H., *Who Stole Feminism? How women have betrayed women* (London: Simon & Schuster, 1995).

10 Wolf, N., *The Beauty Myth: How images of beauty are used against women* (Toronto: Vintage Books, 1990).

11 Sommers, C. H., *Who Stole Feminism?*

12 Khan, M. (ed.), *It's Not About the Burqa: Muslim women on faith, feminism, sexuality and race* (London: Picador, 2020).

13 Barr, B. A., *The Making of Biblical Womanhood: How the subjugation of women became gospel truth* (Grand Rapids, MI: Brazos Press, 2021).

14 Du Mez, K. K., 'Hey, John MacArthur. You have a Culture. It's Called White (Christian) Patriarchy', Kristin Kobes Du Mez, 24 October 2019: https://kristindumez.com/resources/hey-john-macarthur-you-have-a-culture-its-called-white-christian-patriarchy (accessed 14 December 2023).

15 McDonald, C., *God Is Not a White Man: And other revelations* (London: Hodder & Stoughton, 2021).

16 Bauman, C. A., *Theology of the Womb: Knowing God through the body of a woman* (Eugene, OR: Cascade Books, 2019).

17 Buckley, A. R., 'What Does It Mean to be a Christian Feminist?', Relevant, 2022: https://relevantmagazine.com/faith/what-does-it-look-be-christian-feminist (accessed 18 October 2023).

18 'Women and the Imago Dei: Gender Ontology in St. Augustine's Thought', *Res Cogitans* Vol. 8, Issue 1, article 8.

19 Kristof, N. D. and WuDunn, S., *Half the Sky: How to change the world* (London: Virago, 2010).

20 Armas, K., *Abuelita Faith: What women on the margins teach us about wisdom, persistence and strength* (Grand Rapids, MI: Brazos Press, 2021).

Feminism: an incomplete – and tongue-in-cheek – history

1 Gilbert, S. F., *Developmental Biology*, 6th edn (Sunderland, MA: Sinauer Associates, 2000).

2 Greer, G., *The Female Eunuch*.

3 Greer, G., *The Female Eunuch*.

4 Hooks, B., *Feminist Theory: From margin to center* (London: Pluto Press, 2000), p.19.

5 'Conscience payouts to priests top £26m', *Church Times*, 2006: https://www.churchtimes.co.uk/articles/2004/20-february/news/uk/conscience-payouts-to-priests-top-26m (accessed 18 October 2023).

6 'US election: Full transcript of Donald Trump's obscene videotape', BBC, 2016: https://www.bbc.co.uk/news/election-us-2016-37595321 (accessed 18 October 2023).

7 Park, A., '#MeToo reaches 85 countries with 1.7M tweets', CBS News, 24 October 2017: https://www.cbsnews.com/news/metoo-reaches-85-countries-with-1-7-million-tweets (accessed 18 October 2023).

Why I'm not a feminist

1 'Catechism of the Catholic Church', Catholic Culture: https://www.catholicculture.org/culture/library/catechism/index.cfm?recnum=5326 (accessed 22 November 2023).

2 'Catechism of the Catholic Church', Catholic Culture: https://www.catholicculture.org/culture/library/catechism/cat_view.cfm?recnum=5441 (accessed 22 November 2023).

3 Hooper J. and Revill, R., 'A woman's place is to wait and listen, says the Vatican', 1 August 2004: https://www.theguardian.com/world/2004/aug/01/religion.uk (accessed 22 November 2023).

4 'Letter to the Bishops of the Catholic Church on the Collaboration of Men and Women in the Church and in the World', Holy See: https://www.vatican.va/roman_curia/congregations/cfaith/documents/rc_con_cfaith_doc_20040731_collaboration_en.html (accessed 22 November 2023).

Women in pain

1 Tunks, E. Bellissimo and Roy, R., *Chronic Pain: Psychosocial factors in rehabilitation* (Malabar, FL: Krieger Publishing, 1990).

2 'Researcher says women less likely to get painkillers', UPI archives, 11 March 1989: https://www.upi.com/Archives/1989/03/11/Researcher-says-women-less-likely-to-get-painkillers/2047605595600 (accessed 18 October 2023).

3 Fassler, J., 'How Doctors Take Women's Pain Less Seriously', *The Atlantic*, 15 October 2015: https://www.theatlantic.com/health/archive/2015/10/emergency-room-wait-times-sexism/410515 (accessed 18 October 2023).

4 'Women and pain: Disparities in experience and treatment', Harvard Health Publishing, 9 October 2017: https://www.health.harvard.edu/blog/women-and-pain-disparities-in-experience-and-treatment-2017100912562 (accessed 18 October 2023).

5 Greer, G., *The Female Eunuch*.

6 Perez, C. C., *Invisible Women: Exposing data bias in a world made for men* (London: Chatto & Windus, 2019).

7 McDuffee, T., 'We Were Women Comforted by Shared Pain', *Christianity Today*, 13 December 2018: https://www.christianitytoday.com/ct/2018/december-web-only/women-comforted-by-shared-pain-fibromyalgia-refugee.html (accessed 18 October 2023).

8 Gammoh, O. S., 'Fibromyalgia prevalence, treatment trends and correlation with Insomnia among female refugees: Alarming results', *Journal of Neurology & Neurophysiology*, International Online Medical Council (IOMC), 22 August 2016.

9 Singhal, A., Tien, Y.-Y. and Hsia, R.Y., 'Racial-Ethnic Disparities in Opioid Prescriptions at Emergency Department Visits for Conditions Commonly Associated with Prescription Drug Abuse', PLOS ONE, 8 August 2016: https://doi.org/10.1371/journal.pone.0159224 (accessed 18 October 2023).

10 Hoffman, K. M., Trawalter, S., Axt, J. R. and Oliver, M. N., 'Racial bias in pain assessment and treatment recommendations, and false beliefs about biological differences between blacks and whites', Proceedings of the National Academy of Sciences, 4 April 2016: https://doi.org/10.1073/pnas.1516047113 (accessed 18 October 2023).

11 'Menstrual leave – a (period) pain for employers or a positive step to keep people who menstruate in the workplace?', Browne Jacobson, 8 June 2022: https://www.brownejacobson.com/training-and-resources/resources/legal-updates/2022/06/menstrual-leave (accessed 18 October 2023).

12 Greer, G., *The Female Eunuch*.

Female competition – in search of world peace

1 Davis, E. F., *Proverbs, Ecclesiastes, and the Song of Songs* (Louisville, KY: Westminster John Knox, 2000).

2 Held Evans, R., *A Year of Biblical Womanhood: How a liberated woman found herself sitting on her roof, covering her head, and calling her husband master* (Nashville, TN: Thomas Nelson, 2012), p. 76.

Boys will *not* be boys

1 Clinton, T. and Davis, M., *Take It Back*.

2 Cosper, M., 'The Rise and Fall of Mars Hill', episode 4 podcast transcript, Christianity Today, 14 July 2021: https://www.christianitytoday.com/ct/podcasts/rise-and-fall-of-mars-hill/mars-hill-mark-driscoll-podcast-jacks-raging-bile.html (accessed 15 December 2023).

3 Peterson, J. B., 'Men have to toughen up', Twitter, 3 May 2022: https://twitter.com/jordanbpeterson/status/1521500593394696192 (accessed 18 October 2023).

4 Bates, L., *Men Who Hate Women: From incels to pickup artists, the truth about extreme misogyny and how it affects us all* (London: Simon & Schuster, 2020).

5 Rosenberg, E., 'He's pro-incest, pedophilia, and rape. He's also running for Congress from his parents' house', *The Washington Post*, 2 June 2018: https://www.washingtonpost.com/news/local/wp/2018/06/01/hes-pro-incest-pedophilia-and-rape-hes-also-running-for-congress-from-his-parents-house (accessed 18 October 2023).

6 Zand, B., *The Secret World of Incels: UNTOLD*, Channel 4, 14 November 2022.

7 Byrd, A., *Recovering from Biblical Manhood & Womanhood*, p. 22.

8 Malonda-Vidal, E., Samper-García, P., Llorca-Mestre, A., Muñoz-Navarro, R. and Mestre-Escrivá, V., 'Traditional Masculinity and Aggression in Adolescence: Its relationship with emotional processes', *International Journal of Environmental Research and Public Health*, 17 September 2021: https://www.ncbi.nlm.nih.gov/pmc/articles/PMC8469901 (accessed 20 December 2023).

9 Pappas, S., 'American Psychological Association issues first-ever

guidelines for practice with men and boys', January 2019: https://www.apa.org/monitor/2019/01/ce-corner (accessed 18 October 2023).

10 Ngozi Adichie, C., *We Should All be Feminists* (New York: Fourth Estate, 2014).

11 Clinton, T. and Davis, M., *Take It Back*.

Our Mother who art in heaven

1 Young, Wm P., *The Shack* (London: Hodder & Stoughton, 2008).

2 Mettler, K., 'Why God is a curvy, black woman in "The Shack" and some Christian critics say it's "heresy"', *Chicago Tribune*, 2016: https://www.chicagotribune.com/entertainment/movies/ct-god-black-woman-shack-20161221-story.html (accessed 18 October 2023).

3 McDonald, C., *God Is Not a White Man*.

4 Bauman, C. A., *Theology of the Womb*.

5 McDonald, C., 'Why I've stopped using male pronouns for God', Premier Christianity, 2022: https://www.premierchristianity.com/opinion/why-ive-stopped-using-male-pronouns-for-god/13174.article (accessed 18 October 2023).

Women in church leadership: heroes or heretics?

1 Barr, B. A., *The Making of Biblical Womanhood*.

2 Mary McAleese, *Forbes* magazine, 2005: https://www.forbes.com/profile/mary-mcaleese/?sh=287a7bef7c96 (accessed 18 October 2023).

3 Sieghart, M. A., *The Authority Gap: Why women are still taken less seriously than men and what we can do about it* (New York: Doubleday, 2021).

4 Armas, K., *Abuelita Faith*.

5 Both examples taken from Sieghart, M. A., *The Authority Gap*.

6 Goodchild, S., 'Church pays millions to clergy who walked out over women priests', *The Independent*, 10 March 2002: https://www.independent.co.uk/news/uk/home-news/church-pays-millions-to-clergy-who-walked-out-over-women-priests-9196207.html (accessed 15 December 2023).

7 Wallace, G., 'Defusing the 1 Timothy 2:12 Bomb: What Does Paul Mean by Authority (Authentein)?', Junia Project, 12 February

2014: https://juniaproject.com/defusing-1-timothy-212-authority-authentein (accessed 18 October 2023).

8 'Women in Ministry – Dr. Sandra Richter': https://www.youtube.com/watch?v=tpmtq-ZsqC4.

9 Gaventa, B. R., 'Gendered Bodies and the Body of Christ', in *Practicing with Paul: Reflections on Paul and the practices of ministry in honor of Susan G. Eastman*, ed. Burroughs, P. R. (Eugene, OR: Cascade Books, 2018), p. 55.

10 Barr, B. A., *The Making of Biblical Womanhood*, pp. 62–3.

11 Gates, M., *The Moment of Lift: How empowering women changes the world* (New York: Flatiron Books, 2019).

12 Armas, K., *Abuelita Faith*.

13 Byrd, A., *Recovering from Biblical Manhood & Womanhood*, p. 57.

Don't whistle while we work

1 Sieghart, M. A., *The Authority Gap*.

2 O'Connell, E. M., 1 September 2020: https://twitter.com/i_Lean/status/1300661770005049346 (accessed 18 October 2023).

3 McCarty, J., 2021: https://www.linkedin.com/posts/thefemalelead_at-a-nasa-earth-meeting-10-years-ago-a-white-activity-6823603828819025920-sv6j/?trk=public_profile_like_view (accessed 18 October 2023).

4 Solnit, R., *Men Explain Things to Me* (Chicago, IL: Haymarket Books, 2015).

5 Hauser, C., 'Black Doctor Says Delta Flight Attendant Rejected Her; Sought "Actual Physician"', the *New York Times*, 14 October 2016: https://www.nytimes.com/2016/10/15/us/black-doctor-says-delta-flight-attendant-brushed-her-aside-in-search-of-an-actual-physician.html.

6 Armas, K., *Abuelita Faith*.

7 Cotton, B., 'Women account for just 6% of FTSE 100 CEOs – and are paid far less', Business Leader, 8 March 2021: https://www.businessleader.co.uk/women-account-for-just-6-of-ftse-100-ceos-and-are-paid-far-less (accessed 18 October 2023).

8 Chamorro-Premuzic, T., 'Why Do So Many Incompetent Men

Become Leaders?' Harvard Business Review, 22 August 2013: https://hbr.org/2013/08/why-do-so-many-incompetent-men (accessed 18 October 2023).

9 'Nearly two in three young women have experienced sexual harassment at work, TUC survey reveals', TUC, 10 August 2016: https://www.tuc.org.uk/news/nearly-two-three-young-women-have-experienced-sexual-harassment-work-tuc-survey-reveals (accessed 18 October 2023).

10 Bates, L., *Men Who Hate Women*.

11 Bates, L., *Men Who Hate Women*.

12 Bates, L., *Men Who Hate Women*.

13 Martinsen, Ø. L., 'Personality for Leadership', BI Business Review, 20 March 2014: https://www.bi.edu/research/business-review/articles/2014/03/personality-for-leadership (accessed 18 October 2023).

14 Abouzahr, K., Krentz, M., Harthorne, J. and Brooks Taplett, F., 'Why Women-Owned Startups Are a Better Bet', BCG Global, 6 June 2018: https://www.bcg.com/publications/2018/why-women-owned-startups-are-better-bet (accessed 18 October 2023).

15 Dizikes, P., 'Putting heads together', Massachusetts Institute of Technology, 1 October 2010: https://news.mit.edu/2010/collective-intel-1001 (accessed 18 October 2023).

16 Phillips, K., 'Embracing the "socially distinct" outsider' Kellogg School of Management, 7 April 2009: http://www.kellogg.northwestern.edu/news_articles/2009/philipsresearch.aspx (accessed 18 October 2023).

Love, honour and no way

1 Windle, L., *Notes on Love: Being single and dating in a marriage obsessed church* (London: SPCK, 2021).

2 Ngozi Adichie, C., *We Should All be Feminists*.

3 Barr, B. A., *The Making of Biblical Womanhood*.

4 Luther, M., *Luther's Works*: XII, 94, 20–22, Weimar edn (1523).

5 Christians for Biblical Equality, CBE International: cbeinternational.org.

6 Pressley, C., 'Marriage: A Creation Gift', CBMW, 8 October 2021: https://cbmw.org/2021/10/08/danvers-audio-marriage-a-creation-gift-by-clint-pressley (accessed 18 December 2023).

7 Warnock, A., 'Gender: Complementarian vs Egalitarian Spectrum', 24 September 2012: https://www.patheos.com/blogs/adrianwarnock/2012/09/gender-roles-a-complementarian-and-egalitarian-spectrum (accessed 18 October 2023).

8 Stetzer, E., 'Complementarians in Closed Rooms', Church Leaders, 23 June 2020: https://churchleaders.com/pastors/pastor-articles/377746-complementarians-in-closed-rooms.html/2 (accessed 18 October 2023).

9 Kobes Du Mez, K., *Jesus and John Wayne: How white evangelicals corrupted a faith and fractured a nation* (New York: Liveright, 2021).

10 Luther, M., *Luther's Works*: 20:84, Erlangen edn (1522).

11 'Data Matters – Every Woman Matters', Femicide Census, 2015: https://www.femicidecensus.org/data-matters-every-woman-matters (accessed 18 October 2023).

Women in the word

1 Mathews, A., *Gender Roles and the People of God: Rethinking what we were taught about men and women in the Church* (Grand Rapids, MI: Zondervan, 2017).

2 Barr, B. A., *The Making of Biblical Womanhood*.

3 Barr, B. A., *The Making of Biblical Womanhood*.

4 Peppiatt, L., cited in Barr, B. A., *The Making of Biblical Womanhood*.

5 Pope John Paul II, 'Apostolic Letter Mulieris Dignitatem of the Supreme Pontiff John Paul II on the Dignity and Vocation of Women on the Occasion of the Marian Year', The Holy See, 1988: https://www.vatican.va/content/john-paul-ii/en/apost_letters/1988/documents/hf_jp-ii_apl_19880815_mulieris-dignitatem.html (accessed 23 November 2023).

6 The Marriage Course: themarriagecourse.org.

7 Keller, T. and Keller, K., *The Meaning of Marriage: Facing the complexities of commitment with the wisdom of God* (New York: Penguin, 2013).

8 Musters, C. and Musters, S., *Grace-Filled Marriage: Strengthened and*

transformed through God's redemptive love (Milton Keynes: Authentic Media, 2021).

9 Fredericks, K. and Fredericks, M., *Marriage Be Hard* (Colorado Springs, CO: Convergent Books, 2022).

Happy families

1 Tamas, J., 'Breastfeeding maths', 2017: https://www.instagram.com/thejennytamas (accessed 18 October 2023).

2 Frazier, A., 'This Mom Calculated How Much Time She's Spent Breastfeeding In A Year & Yeah, It's *A LOT*', Romper, 17 November 2017: https://www.romper.com/p/this-mom-figured-out-how-many-hours-shes-spent-breastfeeding-in-1-year-spoiler-alert-its-a-lot-5495036 (accessed 18 October 2023).

3 'Husbands create 7 hours of extra housework a week: study', Reuters, 4 April 2008: https://www.reuters.com/article/us-housework-husbands-idUSN0441782220080404 (accessed 18 October 2023).

4 Dunatchik, A. and Özcan, B., 'Reducing mommy penalties with daddy quotas', Journal of European Social Policy, 10 November 2020: https://journals.sagepub.com/doi/abs/10.1177/0958928720963324 (accessed 18 October 2023).

5 Petts, R. J., Knoester, C. and Waldfogel, J., 'Fathers' Paternity Leave-Taking and Children's Perceptions of Father–Child Relationships in the United States'. Sex Roles, February 2020: https://pubmed.ncbi.nlm.nih.gov/32076360 (accessed 18 October 2023).

6 Hodson, P., *Men: An investigation into the emotional male* (London: BBC Books, 1984).

7 Lukits, A., 'Dads' Housework Inspires Girls' Ambitions', *Wall Street Journal*, 18 August 2014: https://www.wsj.com/articles/dads-housework-inspires-girls-ambitions-1408400179 (accessed: 11 October 2023).

Angry men

1 Ling, T. and Saunders, T. 'Top 10: World's most dangerous animals', BBC Science Focus, 20 November 2023: https://www.sciencefocus.com/nature/what-animals-kills-the-most-people (accessed 18 October 2023).

2 Dearden, L., '93% of killers in England and Wales are men, official figures show', *Independent*, 11 March 2021: https://www. independent.co.uk/news/uk/crime/women-murders-men-ons-sarah-everard-b1815779.html (accessed 18 October 2023).

3 Berke, D. S. and Zeichner, A., 'Man's heaviest burden: A review of contemporary paradigms and new directions for understanding and preventing masculine aggression', 2016, *Social and Personality Psychology Compass, 10*(2), pp. 83–91.

4 'Femicide: Women are most likely to be killed by their partner or ex', BBC News, 20 February 2020: https://www.bbc.co.uk/news/ newsbeat-51572665 (accessed 18 October 2023).

5 Bates, L., *Men Who Hate Women*.

6 Huff-Corzine, L. and Marvell, T., 'Domestic Violence and Mass Shootings: A Review of Current Academic Literature', Office of Justice Programs, December 2021: https://www.ojp.gov/pdffiles1/nij/ grants/303499.pdf (accessed 18 October 2023).

7 French, M., *The War Against Women* (New York: Ballantine Books: 1993).

A womb with a view: the way we look at women

1 Sieghart, M. A., *The Authority Gap*.

2 McDonald, C., *God Is Not a White Man*.

3 Brown, A., '"Least Desirable"? How Racial Discrimination Plays Out In Online Dating', NPR, 9 January 2018: https://www.npr. org/2018/01/09/575352051/least-desirable-how-racial-discrimination-plays-out-in-online-dating (accessed 18 October 2023).

4 Piper, J. and Grudem, W. A., *Recovering Biblical Manhood & Womanhood*.

5 Rahman, M. and Berenson, A. B., 'Racial difference in lean mass distribution among reproductive-aged women', National Library of Medicine, 1 October 2011: https://www.ncbi.nlm.nih.gov/pmc/ articles/PMC3076634 (accessed: 18 October 2023).

6 Lundgaard, K., *The Enemy Within: Straight talk about the power and defeat of sin* (Phillipsburg, NJ: P&R Publishing, 1998).

7 Armas, K., *Abuelita Faith*.

8 Tam, A., '"Can I check?" 12 weeks after giving birth, Victoria

Beckham was weighed on live TV', Mamamia, 18 March 2022: https://www.mamamia.com.au/victoria-beckham-weight (accessed 18 October 2023).

9 Iaccino, L., 'Wives are "Penis Homes": Five controversial quotes by Mars Hill Church pastor Mark Driscoll', International Business Times UK, 10 September 2014: https://www.ibtimes.co.uk/wives-are-penis-homes-five-controversial-quotes-by-mars-hill-church-pastor-mark-driscoll-1464881 (accessed 18 October 2023).

10 Peace, M., *The Excellent Wife: A biblical perspective* (Bemidji, MN: Focus Publishing, 1996).

11 ASPS National Clearinghouse of Plastic Surgery Procedural Statistics, 'Plastic Surgery Statistics Report', American Society of Plastic Surgeons, 2018: https://www.plasticsurgery.org/documents/News/Statistics/2018/plastic-surgery-statistics-full-report-2018.pdf (accessed 18 October 2023).

12 Fight the New Drug: fightthenewdrug.org.

13 'How porn affects your sex life', Salt, 4 March 2022: https://www.youtube.com/watch?v=gELYfhv3Ukc (accessed 18 October 2023).

14 Somers, M., 'More than half of Christian men admit to watching pornography', *The Washington Times*, 24 August 2014: https://www.washingtontimes.com/news/2014/aug/24/more-than-half-of-christian-men-admit-to-watching- (accessed 18 October 2023).

15 Gilkerson, L., 'Why are so many Christians addicted to porn?', Covenant Eyes, 19 March 2020: https://www.covenanteyes.com/2009/11/24/why-are-so-many-christians-addicted-to-porn (accessed 18 October 2023).

Sexual healing

1 Piatt, C., 'Mark Driscoll's Oral Fixation', Patheos, 30 April 2013: https://www.patheos.com/blogs/christianpiatt/2013/04/mark-driscolls-oral-fixation (accessed 18 October 2023).

2 Cosper, M., 'The Things We Do to Women', *Christianity Today*, 26 July 2021: https://www.christianitytoday.com/ct/podcasts/rise-and-fall-of-mars-hill/mars-hill-mark-driscoll-podcast-things-we-do-women.html (accessed 18 October 2023).

3 Pearl, D., *Created to Be His Help Meet: Discover how God can make your marriage glorious* (Lobelville, TN: No Greater Joy Ministries, 2004).

4 'A Guide to Marital Rape Law', Noble Solicitors: https://www.noblesolicitors.co.uk/about/a-guide-to-marital-rape.html (accessed: 18 October 2023).

5 Zakaria, R., *Against White Feminism* (London: Hamish Hamilton, 2021).

6 Sommers, C., *Who Stole Feminism?*.

7 Hills, R., *The Sex Myth: The gap between our fantasies and reality* (New York: Simon & Schuster Paperbacks, 2015).

8 Perry, L., *The Case Against the Sexual Revolution: A new guide to sex in the 21st century* (London: Polity, 2022).

9 Harper, K., *From Shame to Sin: The Christian transformation of sexual morality in Late Antiquity* (Harvard University Press, 2013).

10 Kay, A., *This Is Going to Hurt: Secret diaries of a junior doctor* (London: Picador, 2018).

11 Bauman, C. A., *Theology of the Womb*, p. 13.

12 Held Evans, R., *A Year of Biblical Womanhood*.

13 Lockshin, M., 'Onah: A Husband's Conjugal Duties?', TheTorah.com: https://www.thetorah.com/article/onah-a-husbands-conjugal-duties (accessed: 12 October 2023).

Women and sporting bodies – Abigail Irozuru

1 Richards-Ross, S., *Chasing Grace: What the quarter mile has taught me about God and life* (Grand Rapids, MI: Zondervan, 2017).

#ChurchToo

1 Demant, T., 'Rape of Native Women', Amnesty USA: https://bidenhumanrightspriorities.amnestyusa.org/rape-of-native-women (accessed 18 October 2023).

2 Institute for Women's Policy Research: iwpr.org.

3 Green, S., 'Violence Against Black Women – Many Types, Far-reaching Effects', Institute for Women's Policy Research, 13 July 2017: https://iwpr.org/violence-against-black-women-many-types-far-reaching-effects (accessed 19 October 2023).

4 'Black Women & Sexual Violence', National Organisation for
Women: https://now.org/wp-content/uploads/2018/02/Black-Women-
and-Sexual-Violence-6.pdf (accessed 19 October 2023).

5 Hulley, J., Bailey, L., Kirkman, G., Gibbs, G. R., Gomersall, T., Latif,
A. and Jones, A., 'Intimate Partner Violence and Barriers to Help-
Seeking Among Black, Asian, Minority Ethnic and Immigrant
Women: A Qualitative Metasynthesis of Global Research', Sage
Journals, 2 February 2022: https://journals.sagepub.com/doi/
full/10.1177/15248380211050590 (accessed 19 October 2023).

6 Barlow, J. N., 'Black women, the forgotten survivors of sexual assault',
American Psychological Association, 1 February 2020: https://www.
apa.org/topics/sexual-assault-harassment/black-women-sexual-
violence (accessed 19 October 2023).

7 Eligon, J., '"You're Not Supposed to Betray Your Race": The Challenge
Faced by Black Women Accusing Black Men', the *New York Times*,
22 March 2019: https://www.nytimes.com/2019/03/22/us/meredith-
watson-duke-justin-fairfax.html (accessed 20 December 2023).

8 Bluhm, T., *Prey Tell: Why we silence women who tell the truth and
how everyone can speak up* (Grand Rapids, MI: Brazos Press, 2021).

9 Dewan, S., 'Why Women Can Take Years to Come Forward With
Sexual Assault Allegations', *The New York Times*, 19 September 2018:
https://www.nytimes.com/2018/09/18/us/kavanaugh-christine-blasey-
ford.html (accessed 20 December 2023).

10 Bates, L., *Men Who Hate Women*.

11 Paglia, C., 'Opinion | Madonna – Finally, a Real Feminist', the
New York Times, 14 December 1990: https://www.nytimes.
com/1990/12/14/opinion/madonna-finally-a-real-feminist.html
(accessed 20 December 2023).

12 Roiphe, K., 'Date Rape's Other Victim', the *New York Times*, 13 June
1993: https://www.nytimes.com/1993/06/13/magazine/date-rape-s-
other-victim.html (accessed 20 December 2023).

13 Bates, L., *Men Who Hate Women*.

14 Lee, G., 'Men are more likely to be raped than be falsely
accused of rape', FactCheck, Channel 4 News, 12 October
2018: https://www.channel4.com/news/factcheck/

factcheck-men-are-more-likely-to-be-raped-than-be-falsely-accused-of-rape (accessed 19 October 2023).

15 Criminal Injuries Helpline, 'Sexual Assault & Rape Statistics – 2023 UK Data', 1 January 2023: https://criminalinjurieshelpline.co.uk/blog/sexual-assault-data-stats (accessed 19 October 2023).

16 'Read Rachael Denhollander's full victim impact statement about Larry Nassar', CNN, 24 January 2018: https://edition.cnn.com/2018/01/24/us/rachael-denhollander-full-statement/index.html (accessed 19 October 2023).

17 Barr, B. A., *The Making of Biblical Womanhood*.

18 Bluhm, T., *Prey Tell*.

19 Heminsley, A., *Some Body to Love: A family story* (London: Arrow, 2022).

20 Armas, K., *Abuelita Faith*.

21 Bluhm, T., *Prey Tell*.

Why Christians don't believe women who speak up – Tiffany Bluhm

1 Daly, M., *Beyond God the Father: Toward a philosophy of women's liberation* (Boston: Beacon Press, 1992).

2 Josephus, *Antiquities of the Jews* 4.219, in Flavius Josephus, *The Works of Flavius Josephus*, trans. William Whiston (1895).

3 Bluhm, T., *Prey Tell*.

What Christians (men and women) can do next

1 Gates, M., *The Moment of Lift*, p. 258.

2 Rohr, R., 'Trust and Surrender', Center for Action and Contemplation, 7 March 2017: https://cac.org/daily-meditations/trust-and-surrender-2017-03-07 (accessed 19 October 2023).

3 Bates, L., *Men Who Hate Women*.

4 Sieghart, M. A., *The Authority Gap*.

5 Bazelon, E., 'A Seat at the Head of the Table', the *New York Times Magazine*, 21 February 2019: https://www.nytimes.com/interactive/2019/02/21/magazine/women-corporate-america.html (accessed 17 December 2023).

6 Sieghart, M. A., *The Authority Gap*.

7 Zundel, V., '7 out of 10 female Christians believe women should be allowed into church leadership, survey reveals', *Woman Alive*, 24 March 2022: https://www.womanalive.co.uk/opinion/7-out-of-10-female-christians-believe-women-should-be-allowed-into-church-leadership-survey-reveals/12690.article (accessed 19 October 2023).

8 Tannehill, B., '10 Ways Right-Wing Christians Are Destroying Christianity', *HuffPost*, 6 December 2017: https://www.huffpost.com/entry/10-ways-christians-are-destroying-christianity_b_8213708 (accessed 19 October 2023).

9 Armas, K., *Abuelita Faith*.

10 Flood, A., 'Jimmy Carter rails against worldwide "abuse of women and girls" in new book', *The Guardian*, 24 March 2014: https://www.theguardian.com/books/2014/mar/24/jimmy-carter-call-to-action-women-girls-abuse (accessed 19 October 2023).

11 Gates, M., *The Moment of Lift*.

12 Windle, L., *Notes on Love*.

13 Bauman, C. A., *Theology of the Womb*.

14 Barr, B. A., *The Making of Biblical Womanhood*.

A litany to honor women

1 'A Litany to Honor Women' in Claiborne, S., Wilson-Hartgrove J. and Okoro, E., *A Litany for Ordinary Radicals* (Grand Rapids, MI: Zondervan, 2010).

And finally…

1 Bennett, A., *Our Women: Chapters on the sex-discord* (New York: Doran, 1920), p. 112.

2 Barr, B. A., *The Making of Biblical Womanhood*.

3 Byrd, A., *Recovering from Biblical Manhood & Womanhood*.

4 Held Evans, R., *A Year of Biblical Womanhood*.

5 Armas, K., 'A Legacy of Survival', Plough, 22 November 2022: https://www.plough.com/en/topics/life/relationships/a-legacy-of-survival (accessed 17 December 2022).

6 Sieghart, M. A., *The Authority Gap*.

'Wonderfully insightful, uncomfortably challenging and hilariously amusing'
J John

Being single and dating in a marriage obsessed church

NOTES ON LOVE

LAUREN WINDLE

If you enjoyed this book, check out Lauren's first book, *Notes on Love: Being Single and Dating in a Marriage Obsessed Church*. The following excerpt will give you a glimpse of how Lauren deals with this important subject matter with her characteristic frankness and humour.

Things we shouldn't say to single people (and some suggested responses)

Why aren't you married? You're attractive, funny and clever.
Yeh, I'm actually overqualified.

I know you're single, but here's a plus one to my wedding anyway.
Great, I'll bring Sydney from accounting, who will be in your wedding photos (but not my life) for all eternity.

We're all sharing with our other halves for this weekend. Who are you sharing with?
Me? I'll be paying the single-occupancy rate and face-planting the mini bar.

So when's it your turn to settle down and get married?
I'm not sure. I did take a ticket when I came in, but I think I may have missed them calling my number when I nipped to the loo.

Just use this time to work on yourself.
I can't wait till I'm married when I don't need to do any personal development of any kind.

You'll find someone.
This is life, John. Not a giant game of hide-and-seek.

Jesus is your lover.
Thanks, well-meaning person I don't know that well in church. While Jesus is great, there are still some specifically human desires I'm hoping to satisfy this side of glory.

Are you getting yourself out there?
If I can get the coordinates for 'out there', I'll head over right now.

Awww, I'm sorry to hear you're single.
Could you pop that into a get-well-soon card with a 'cheer-me-up' fiver?

If you're still single by 30 you should freeze your eggs.
Cheers, Mum. Would a puppy satiate your desire for grandchildren?